NATURALIST'S
JOURNAL

A
NATURALIST'S
JOURNAL

M. YUVAN

Foreword by
G. Gautama

Edited by
Charles Lawrence and Helen Lawrence

Notion Press

Old No. 38, New No. 6
McNichols Road, Chetpet
Chennai - 600 031

First Published by Notion Press 2017
Copyright © M. Yuvan 2017
All Rights Reserved.

ISBN 978-1-947752-50-4

For my Mother and little sister

CONTENTS

AUTHOR'S NOTE

All the essays I have penned for this book are the result of numerous Nature walks I have gone on; with children, with friends, with colleagues and many alone. More than bringing me to understand the lives of butterflies, birds, snakes and other creatures, walks for me have been a journey of self-discovery and a way of connecting with the earth and with life. Walks have helped me dissolve the distinction between myself and the larger environment, between the mindscape and the landscape. And the act of walking has allowed me to witness the world around and grow more aware of the sensations and currents within me. And I have learnt much from simple acts such as sitting by a plant and watching it for some time every day, strolling through paddyfields, listening to bird song and routinely looking beneath leaves. All the photographs appearing here too are ones I took during these pursuits.

Many of the writings here are set in the landscape in and around Pathashaala, the Krishnamurti School I studied in and worked in for some time. Pathashaala is a large residential campus situated deep in the countryside of Tamil Nadu, surrounded by *eris* (man made lakes), vast expanses of paddy fields and other cultivations, hills and scrublands. This is the space where much of who I am and what I believe in and stand for, emerged and took shape. It is a place whose memories and people I will always hold as precious and draw strength from. There are some essays which are before and after my time at Pathashaala.

What I wish to share through my writing is more than just anecdotes and observations on the various forms of life you will encounter as you sift through these pages. These are wanderings, ponderings, insights, reflections, fond recollections and the stories I hold special and I wish to tell. But more than anything these essays are an invitation, a joyous and heartfelt invitation to anyone who may read them, to be deeply in touch with the entire abounding community of life around.

M. Yuvan

FOREWORD

The first work of an author is always special and contains glimpses of future journeys. It is also a telling statement of the journey of the author thus far. For this young author this book is a culmination of one phase of his journey, and entering the stream of adulthood with responsibility, dignity and wider landscapes. It is with deep happiness that I write this introduction to Yuvan's first published work.

As a school Principal, one meets closely with the myriad natures of the human species. One chooses to work with them without choice and without privileging one student over another. The challenge of guiding and nourishing the spirit of each individual is sometimes very difficult, particularly when attempting to meet the academic expectations of society. There is the odd student who makes this job ever more difficult, one who pops up out of the blue with intensity, jagged edges and an interest in wild things. Over thirty years of working with very young people, I have encountered perhaps three or four students who have been deeply interested in snakes - they could see them where none else could. Not only were these characters colorful and full of energy, but also the ones who would know the campus intimately, seeing a forest of hidden creatures where none others saw anything but trees, flowers and a few birds. These students were always special, as their close relationship with the campus and its creatures was a rare and remarkable one. Yuvan has been one of these persistent and eclectic young people – interested in birds and insects and reptiles and plants and butterflies in equal measure.

I have had the special opportunity of watching Yuvan grow from a kindergarten student in The School -KFI to adulthood in Pathashaala (PCFL-KFI). In the younger days, fights with classmates were common and so was 'time out' from class. I remember him walking in and out of school with his sister, and also racing around the school with others in pursuit, or chasing someone. It is the special privilege of childhood that sweetness and mischievous behavior can go hand in hand. And it is the special challenge for educators to hold the mischief in check while not smothering the enormous energy of childhood.

Though Yuvan had held me at a wary distance for most of his early school life, his mother grew to trust the intentions, advice and guidance of the school. And when, at age 16, in Grade 11, Yuvan took the decision to drop out of formal schooling and appear for exams as a private candidate. This opened opportunities that he would otherwise never have had. While he and his mother were thinking about his future, he stayed a few months at Pathashaala, the just-started KFI residential school 75 km from Chennai, near Thirukalukundram. Though he visited the Valley School and Shibumi in Bangalore, Yuvan chose to 'live' in Pathashaala and grew to love its wild, stark beauty. We could not have 'teaching' classes for him as we were a very small young school with students all below 14 years. Intuitively, Yuvan seemed to have felt that Pathashaala would suit him and his mother felt that he would be safe in my care. What a responsibility such simple trust puts on one! And what a blessing and a privilege it is, too!

Pathashaala, the newest of Krishnamurti Foundation India schools, started in 2010. It is an unusual school that tries to offer residents an opportunity to live in an environmentally sustainable manner, conscious of our water, energy, food and sanitation choices. It tries to function with shared ownership of the learning environment where, with the teacher as an educator-learner and the student a learner-educator. Pathashaala explores this symmetry.

Yuvan spent four years in Pathashaala living with a few Learner-Educators, fewer Educator - Learners, joining the initial band of pioneers in a new KFI residential school. One could see his exhilaration as soon as he woke up and was out to explore the grasses, trees, bushes, lakes etc. Soon one of the Educator - Learners helped him purchase a camera and he went about looking for and identifying caterpillars, bugs, worms, snakes, birds, butterflies, trees, ants, grasses and all manner of creatures. "What is this?" Would set him off naming things in English, Tamil and in Latin and sharing stories. He enjoyed a great fan following among the students, as this was not only a fascinating way of learning things for the children but a new dimension of living, too. His explanations were as illustrative as they were entertaining, and his stories and observations, eye opening and evocative.

During this period with the support and guidance of the Educator - Learners resident in Pathashaala and from The School, he was studying Maths, Physics, Chemistry and Biology. These were his formal subjects. Yuvan completed his AS exams and A level exams as an external candidate at HLC and passed his exams creditably. He continued to live in Pathashaala while embarking on a degree course at IGNOU. He was a quasi educator-learner, not yet an adult, nor a formal student. He taught classes and contributed to the outreach work in neighboring village schools by way of conducting science workshops. He spent his time for ruminations, discussions with adults and learning the art of being a teacher. Dubbed 'our resident naturalist' he used his small stipend from Pathashaala to buy books and a good camera. Pathashaala was the soil where his school, college and life's learnings rolled into one harmonious whole, almost like the vast wide skies under which one lives and functions here.

Yuvan was single minded in the pursuit of things and ideas. He played the Recorder (a woodwind instrument) with zeal and passion. Having read that 10,000 hours of practice makes one an expert at anything, he gave himself to this endeavor with enthusiasm, practicing on some days for 14 hours. As a bright young person he reads voraciously and has tried many things. Science and Physics fascinated him as also the human mind. Feynman appealed to him as much as V.S. Ramachandran and Malcolm Gladwell. These are things one would expect to see in any bright young person. However, inspite of strong academic abilities, his quality of observation, particularly of natural phenomena, has been tuned by his readings of M. Krishnan and other eminent naturalists. Learning about oneself and bringing the same sharp observation of nature to one's own deep patterns and conditioning, was a parallel journey for him.

Yuvan had no problem being alone in the campus during the vacations, sharing meals with whoever was resident. In fact he seemed to enjoy these solitary periods as, like Sherlock Holmes, he could pursue undisturbed all manner of investigations. Which plant had leaves eaten more than others? How many types of larvae inhabited a given plant? How do birds chase other birds and how do snakes trap their prey? It was not surprising to find him emerging from behind a tree, or seated patiently in front of a plant for hours, waiting for a butterfly to unfurl its wings.

Life's designs are mysterious. Yuvan has had a most unusual and wonderful education at Pathashaala - adequate support, enough caring attention, and perhaps also benign neglect. All these allowed the larger dimensions of the world to speak to his being.

His wanderings in Pathashaala yielded a booklet of photographs of 80 butterflies and another on 140 birds. He also did a similar documentation for Bhoomi College and the Bhoomi Rainforest Research Station in the Sharavati hills. With this book he moves from budding amateur naturalist to a mature one. It is a fitting recognition that he has just received the prestigious M. Krishnan Nature Writing Award from the Madras Naturalists' Society. His passion for observing and understanding living things is a deep and abiding aspect of his being. He is happy to share his knowledge.

Reading his stories, one may be forgiven for feeling a tinge of envy at his education. The reader will no doubt find the accounts in this book evocative, informative and enjoyable. They will reveal facets of our world we overlook due to our busy, and often unaware, lifestyles. Many of his accounts are as hilarious as they are profound. The stories will also touch long forgotten chords of a fragile kinship that we share with other living creatures. This is a magical space where one species studies and supports other species without judgment, holding the cobra and the scorpion with as much affection as the lark and the caterpillar. This loving embrace of nature and her ways, however mysterious and difficult to comprehend fully, has given Yuvan a rare and privileged location.

J. Krishnamurti pointed to the work of our schools sharply by saying, "If five people turn their back on money and power, you have done your job." It may be difficult to count five. But may be one … It is with happiness and a full heart I wish him and his endeavors a natural and beautiful flowering. One wishes for him a life where he always has the space to walk among nature, observe and document its mysteries.

G. Gautama

Director - Secretary
Palar Centre for Learning
*(Pathashaala, Outreach & Krishnamurti Study
Centre)*
Krishnamurti Foundation India

ACKNOWLEDGEMENTS

I am immensely grateful to G. Gautama, Director - Secretary of The Paalar Centre for Learning (Pathashaala, Outreach and Krishnamurti Study Centre) for inviting me into a rare and extraordinary educational experience and creating the space for me to grow and discover myself.

I am thankful to my mentors K. Ramesh, Uma Iyer, Seetha Ananthasivan, S. Balakrishnan, Sumitra.M. Gautama, Esther Anand, Aravind Venkataraman, Ramkumar Mahadevan, Yasaswani Sampathkumar, Padmavathy Sundararajan, Sonia Aravind, S.N. Sampath, Bina Shivram and Kamala Anilkumar for guiding me, encouraging me, supporting me and opening doors for me at various points of time.

I am extremely thankful to my Uncle and Aunt, Charles Lawrence and Helen Lawrence for editing my manuscript in such meticulous detail and for being there and supporting me during the entire journey of this book.

The gratitude I feel towards my mother is beyond what words can express. Summer or winter, success or severe hardship, together or apart, she is the sole person who has always been there for me, trusted in me, nurtured me and stood by me, and I know she always will.

BEL PLANTS AND LIME CATERPILLARS

JULY NOON. I HAVE COME FOR A DE-STRESSING stroll in the herb garden after a morning packed with classes with the junior kids. The intensity of the summer sun bears its traces even till now. As I had been anticipating, my wandering gaze notices a single Lime butterfly meandering about in the garden with an air of purpose. Very soon it is going to lay its eggs on the Bel saplings (Aegle marmelos), probably the first clutch for the season. Although their larvae, just like most other ones, are highly choosy about what they eat, the butterflies are pathetic at identifying their host plants by sight. This one I am watching has inspected the Bauhinia and then the Laburnum before it even got close to one of the Bels. A year back, around the same time on a similar walk, I remember another Lime butterfly which paid a visit to the old faded green towel of one of the gardening staff which he had put out on the tall grass for drying, after a bath. Was the butterfly being inquisitive or did it mistake the green threadbare cloth for vegetation? I would argue for the latter as the insect was shortly going to lay its eggs and its inspection of the old towel lasted just for a moment before it flew away in a spurt of apparent realization.

A butterfly's sense of smell is supposedly vastly superior compared to its acuity of vision. But as it is well known, it has its nose (or rather its olfactory organs) on its forelegs. So an egg laying butterfly approaches a plant which it takes for a potential host plant, and then taps its leaves like a Tabla player to identify it from its scent, a behavior aptly named 'Drumming.' After its many trials and disappointments it eventually manages to locate its host plant. Now its drumming increases in tempo and it does a protracted survey of every other leaf on the plant to choose the tender most and best ones for its progeny to devour. The thick, old, infected or bug eaten leaves are avoided almost with a gesture of disgust. Some ovipositing butterflies may spend so much time inspecting and selecting leaves that they have to intermittently visit a patch of Tridax or Pignut flowers nearby to refuel their energy reserves.

This year a gang of Social spiders (Stegodyphus sarasinorum) have spread their webs and have become the new tenants on one of the Bel saplings in the garden. Theirs is a shabby model of housing starting from a central stronghold of dense webbing from which its keepers hardly surface, terminating in random crisscrossing strands scaffolded to the leaves and stems of the plant they choose. These spiders are very fond of constructing their webs on the solar lamps along the pathways in the campus as I think they know they get a more steady supply of insects there. Anyways, the webs are cleared every month or so as they completely block off the light after a point. When an unfortunate insect does get stuck in the strands, most often the arachnids don't seem to be immediately aroused. But the next morning one will note that the prey has promptly been fed on or taken into the larder inside. Other than them a Bully ant colony (Camponotus compressus) has its nest underground among the roots of the Bel plants. They are, as ants by nature are, perpetually busy parading out in search of food, bringing in morsels and pieces and if nothing else, throwing out sanding grains and expanding the nest, which now forms a formidable moat around the sapling. Horned Treehoppers reside all along the stem and live off its sap. They are fiercely protected by the ants in return for the excess sap they exude which the ants graciously ingest as payment for the bodyguard service. These insects unlike their neighbors below hardly show any movement other than when poked, to which in response they will pivot around the stem and continue with their unstriving existence. Now the long vacant top floor of the sapling has been taken over by these spiders.

A Lime butterfly usually will lay its eggs singly under a leaf of its choice or at times on grass or shrubbery close to the plant. This Lime butterfly I am watching now seems to prefer depositing its eggs very close to this new spider web, infact one was laid right on it, leaving it dangling on a strand, even though its legs almost got tangled a few times in the process. The butterfly looked quite deliberate in its actions and this behavior is quite new to me. Probably the arachnids provide free security services for the eggs from parasites and predators. However I will keep a look out for similar behavior henceforth to validate this hypothesis.

This year the Bel plants have grown to about five feet and are dressed in enough leaf cover to withstand another bout of defoliation at the jaws of the gluttonous Lime caterpillars. A couple of years ago, the young saplings would be eaten to almost a bare stump. This butterfly also has a taste for many plants we find edible along with the similar looking caterpillars of the Common Mormon butterfly. The Curry leaf saplings planted every once in a while behind the kitchen never manage to make it to the next year. The Lime tree, just outside the campus, although having been ravaged year after year, has withstood the hardships and now stands quite tall. The caterpillars have no taste for the darker and strong scented leaves of Lime and hence leave them untouched. The younger and tender ones nevertheless are reduced to their midribs. Our country is under the plight of a plethora of invasive species introduced from the New World, ranging from the Prosopis thorns to the pestering Cockroaches but one also hears the woes of Sweet Lime cultivators in the West facing the peril of our very own Lime caterpillars which I suppose have been unexpectedly taken back on return journeys.

The ravenous larvae pay a dear price however when they completely strip very young plants of their foliage. Shortly, Bulbuls and Bee-eaters fly by and pick off almost every last one of the larvae as they are left without any leaf cover to hide beneath. Host plant or host planet, its excessive exploitation turns out to be no path to survival!

The pearly green eggs the insect left behind hatch in a few days. During the first half of their larval lives, the Limes remarkably resemble droppings. Many have written that they look like bird droppings but to me they look more like reptile droppings, say a Skink's, Garden lizard's or a small Keel back's. The humus brown on its head and rear blend into a paler and creamy shade on its torso, a complexion least appealing to anything with an appetite. To take its pretence a trifle further, young caterpillars may often 'drop' to the ground as a reaction to sudden disturbances and lie there for a while motionless, further resembling their object of imitation. Caterpillars of various other butterfly and moth species adopt this method of mimicking something uninteresting or disagreeable (often something found on the ground) and then drop to the ground when a threat is perceived. Another good example would be the caterpillar of the Even-Banded Hawk Moth (Neogurelca hyas). In these parts this caterpillar is a staunch devourer of the Nona tree (Morinda tinctoria). Its color is the dull yellow of a dying leaf about to fall off its stalk. When prodded first, it will retract its limbs and straighten out like a dying leaf. Another touch and it will do a free fall to the ground

I was entrusted with twenty hours of teaching a week whilst living in a residential school while also being a house parent for sixteen stormy teenagers, over and above managing my studies through correspondence in the scant space left in between. And added to this were frequent staff meetings and substitution periods. Under these circumstances I have many a time come to envy a caterpillar's lifestyle. Its primary activity throughout the day is to eat and eat more, interspersing its meals between long siestas under the cool shade of leaves. And by virtue of its gluttony, a caterpillar during its larval life outgrows its skin several times and hence it periodically has to shed it. Immediately after that, it promptly eats that up as well! Having being hauled into teaching in school, even before forming clear thoughts of a career or, at the least, acquiring a degree, left me with a growing feeling of inadequacy. This was especially so in the company of my distinguished colleagues. Caterpillars, butterflies, birds, snakes and the rest of the wilderness the surroundings offered were my necessary diversions to stifle toxic emotions and manage and chug along. But inevitably in my conversations with people this or that species of some kind gets mentioned and are frequently interspersed with a binomial name or two, which alone have got me the respect of a high browed intellectual.

Coming back to the Limes, if at all there is any other exertion it takes upon itself, it is excretion. But do note that as soon as the caterpillar is done with its toilet duties it immediately hurries away from the spot it occupied, even to a different leaf. You don't want your predators to follow the bread crumbs straight to you. Keeping a distance or even the concealment of one's droppings is yet another attribute prevalent not just among insects and their larvae but all creatures that feature in the menu cards of many others. Some like the Moringa Webber and the Awl caterpillars hide their droppings between stitched up leaves. Others like the Geometrid moth larvae point their posteriors so as to make their poop fall right on the ground and not anywhere on the plant. And notice how a Fan-throated lizard frantically scampers away from its scat, the moment it is done with its job. But what I find the most fantastic measure of them all is that of the Katydid. As soon as it relieves itself, the insect perfectly times a powerful back heel kick at the falling pellet, hurling it several feet away!

By the fourth or fifth shed of its outgrown larval skin, the Lime caterpillar undergoes a transformation. Only in appearance though and not in habits. From its earlier fecal brown garb emerges a parrot green creature, nothing less fantastic than a frog turning into a prince. The markings on the mantle of this creature may somewhat make it look snake-like at first glance but not quite later. More serpentine and striking is the semblance of a Hawk Moth's caterpillar which the Lime poorly mimics (if at all it does). One wonders why the larva has evolved such a radical change in its complexion at this stage of its lifecycle. Probably it has become too conspicuous an entity to get away by mimicking droppings for there is hardly a creature around whose droppings span the size the caterpillar now is. And therefore it deems it wise to resort to the good old strategy of camouflage.

There is however another characteristic line of defence the Lime's caterpillar (and of most other Swallowtail butterflies') employs in the face of an imminent threat. The creature curls backwards and a forked blood red organ, like a tongue of a snake, flares out from the top of its head leaving its aggressor surprised for a few moments. In the meantime it tries to get away. During this display you will discover that the creature has also exuded a strange odor, a smell which initially is sweet but then induces slight nausea when over inhaled.

Having gotten used to this behavior, I frequently have this caterpillar amuse my students and fellow colleagues with its antics. The ensuing aroma however wasn't appreciated by many. I was quite curious to find out what effect this nauseous scent has on its real predators. I quickly gave up the idea of waiting around to watch the reactions of a bird which may decide to come and peck it. Instead I held an annoyed caterpillar under the nose of Don, my faithful companion dog, to study his responses. At first he showed no change of expressions but in a few moments the odor reached his olfactories, and made him back away and sneeze a couple of times. That's all, nothing more than that. I suppose that the reactions would have been more graphic in smaller creatures, like a Flycatcher or Bulbul. But on another walk soon after I think I did see Don giving me a skeptical expression when we crossed the Bel plants.

It is also around this time that I schedule the chapter on "A Butterfly's Lifecycle" for the middle school students. From egg to adult, every stage of the Lime and other butterflies or moths are present in the herbal garden. The kids are assigned to look under each leaf of designated plants for eggs, larvae and pupae, note their location and keep an eye on them for a week and record changes. They also put down descriptions of the butterfly species they observe in the field so that they can use it to identify them back in class using a field guide. This I have always found a very engaging activity with new discoveries each time, aside from the little noise and disorder and ambling about, which is to be expected from kids. The class often ends with the Lime caterpillar doing its warning display after being prodded and this unfailingly thrills the children.

When a full grown caterpillar empties a notably copious quantity of its bowels, one knows that it is considering pupation in a short while. It first fixes its rear end like a cantilever and hangs diagonally with two strands of silk securing its torso onto the plant's stem. But I have found Lime pupae on many other unlikely places too like brick piles, electric posts and steel fences to mention a few but as a general rule they always pupate close to the feeding plant. Within a day, the green of the creature starts withering away and the pupa starts resembling a little sea conch. However it is not always that when a caterpillar secures itself in the aforementioned manner that pupation is likely. Several are the times when I have eagerly tracked such caterpillars to document the way the creature transforms, but in a short while they will be seen dawdling about again or taking out another leaf. I have learnt that these larvae too take naps on hot afternoons.

In a couple of months, many lineages of Lime caterpillars would have pupated, emerged as adults, mated and laid eggs again. I suspect that by end of November I would have seen not less than five generations of Limes on the Bel plants. The prancing and panicky flight of the Lime butterflies outnumbers every other Swallowtail butterfly species by far at a certain point of time. Only the first torrents of the Northeast monsoon, followed by the occasional cyclone in December, bring this breeding spree to a halt and I can almost hear the Bel saplings gasp in relief. Many of the adult Limes probably migrate, as their numbers discernibly drop. The remaining ones now keep a low profile during these months of challenging weather. What I also see is that the Bels, in the last couple of years, have grown fast and well. My fingers can barely grasp around their girths near the base. Come summer and it grows an abundant number of fresh trifoliate leaflets on the stem tops along with a formidable number of thorns on the younger branches. And I wonder if the adversity they face for these few months has played a role in making them grow hardier and thrive during the rest of the year.

THE SONG OF A WHISTLING THRUSH

I CANNOT FORGET MY FIRST ENCOUNTER WITH the Malabar Whistling Thrush. It was when I was in Grade Nine, while I was on a school trip with the rest of my class to Sholai School. Sholai is a residential campus and an alternate school in Kodaikanal located within the Shola forests. On the first morning, I felt very much adventurous, so I got up silently, tiptoed out of the room and ventured into the forest just beyond the campus property, even before my classmates had their heads out of their sleeping bags. Only after going someway downhill, amongst dense and unfamiliar vegetation, did the anxiety of being reprimanded by my teachers for my irresponsible wandering off, began to creep within me. And either as a consequence or by its own untimely will, nature's call began to increase its throbbing demands. In this situation, close from behind me, came a mellifluous whistle through the mist, so long drawn, so lively, that I didn't think it could have been from a bird or any other creature. It was certainly among the most enchanting sounds I had heard, but yet there was something spooky about it. I wasn't able to trace its source despite looking around and I was growing unsure of which direction the call was coming from, which made it feel all the more eerie to me.

By the time the second whistle had started, my panicked mind began contemplating forest spirits or something else paranormal being at large and responsible for the sound. So I began a brisk stride back to the hostel without looking back. To my relief however I was reassured by a senior student that this was infact the call of a Malabar Whistling Thrush and I myself had the revelation of seeing it the very next morning. Although that did not happen before being given a stern talk by my teachers that day for straying away from the group inspite of instructions.

Far more than its fellow forest birds, the Whistling thrush is very particular about the acoustic quality of its song. It doesn't blare at any time of the day like a barbet just to keep reinstating that it too has a voice. Nor does it relentlessly experiment with new motifs and meters like a Magpie Robin, which ofcourse is another Ustaad among birds. The Whistling Thrush does a professional performance. Firstly it knows very well that any sound carries best and unattenuated in cold and misty air, and hence it renders its song only at dawn. By 9 a.m. the bird wraps up and if at all one hears it later on, it would be a sharp whistle it voices in fright when you unexpectedly stumble upon it at a turning in the forest path or whilst it is being hounded about by a Drongo.

In deep valleys, preferably close to a stream, the bird finds itself a podium, either a boulder or a branch, as the increased humidity around greatly enhances the timbre of its voice. It is also very fond of using the morning fog over inundated paddyfields at the edge of forests to widely propagate its sound and therefore often takes up its residence nearby cultivations.

Coming to its song. The name Whistling school boy which is what it is fondly called as may seem fitting for the bird to a non-musician. But its music is by no means puerile. And although its tune feels free wandering and formless, closer listening will reveal enough features to it that it is worth its own study in musical terms.

This glimmering blue bird is a great improviser and its improvisations closely follow a slow swing style with a generous use of syncopation and some dotted rhythms. Though it largely likes to sing at free tempo, at times its renditions fit well into a 6/8 compound metre. Do clap along and see for yourself. The slurred phrases of its melody are sung with single long breaths which quite often end with an accented high note followed by some subdued lower notes, giving a smooth and unfinished touch to it. On some mornings the bird chooses not to improvise and instead loosely employs the structure of 'Theme and Variation,' an extensively used form among its human counterparts in classical music. The recurring theme though doesn't become evident unless one listens to its song for several minutes.

When one hears the Whistling Thrush for the first time, every one of us is struck by the complexity and the emotional vividity of its song. It is only after many subsequent hearings that the awe elicited by its call wanes and one starts forming deeper and lateral perceptions of it. Atleast, that's how it was for me. It is then when one realizes that the thrush's song infact has a melancholic or even mildly lamenting feel to it.

Sitting at the Bhoomi ashram deep in the Sharavathi hills in the Western Ghats, looking down into a misty valley, I spent many mornings alone attempting to replicate the bird's call on my Recorder (a Woodwind instrument, not a recording device) while the Thrush was singing steeply below me, wanting to see how the bird would respond to this poor mimicry or mockery. It wasn't an entirely futile pursuit though, as from the notes I found myself playing, I discovered that the bird largely sings on a whole tone scale, a musical scale with equal intervals between its notes, which is the reason for the slight gloominess of its tune. And the rising and falling dynamics the bird adorns it with and the extended silences between its passages, add to its mystic quality.

Steep valley…
the crescendo of
a whistling thrush

All this said, I have tried to describe the Malabar Whistling Thrush's musicality from a purely Western musical point of view which is akin to guessing the elephant from one end (Thrush actually). It is very much likely that if enquired through the windows of other forms of music, more interesting aspects of the bird may reveal themselves. Different metaphors uncover different realities. But when speaking of many forms of music, I also wonder if these Thrushes vary in their musical styles across different geographical regions in our country, just like in the case of our own species.

And probably like us, birdsong too evolves with changing times and merges and mixes when different styles amongst them meet. Sometimes, while listening to the bird, my mind brings forth the imagery of a stream flowing in the jungle; fluid, lengthy and changing course. Sometimes I have felt that the undulating hills of the Western Ghats are being portrayed by the Thrush's melody. Quite possibly these are what the bird sings of or what else could it be? The bird must have surely been touched by something beyond itself to sing a song so elaborate and evocative.

A PINK BIRD WITH A PERSONA

SITTING BY A WETLAND, I FIND FEW OTHER WATER birds as entertaining to watch as the lofty necked Flamingos. Do note that here I speak quite apart from their striking colours and general visual appeal. I also speak apart from all the misshapen and clumsy ways they manage to prop themselves up, deserving to have their very own book of Asanas. The American poet Kay Ryan describes the bird rather succinctly as so - "too vivid and peculiar to be pretty and flexible to the point of oddity"

On a usual day of birding at any wetland, all that you may see a Sandpiper do is to routinely scurry on its chosen waterline, repetitiously thrusting its beak into the mud while oscillating its posterior. More patience is required to observe the Grey Heron, which may spend considerable lengths of time watching unwaveringly into the water. One can't help but wonder whether the creature is inspecting for fish or contemplating over its own reflection. Given a whole hour, a group of Grey Herons may have managed to advance only a few feet in the forward direction on their foraging sessions. And one soon grows weary of a large flock of Black Winged Stilts, whose heaving flutter of activity becomes too much to follow for a restless eye.

A flock of Flamingos however have no aspects to them which grow on one to be in any way monotonous. Their lives are as multifaceted as a bird's could be, and in a given flock you can see individuals involved in fighting, foraging, stretching exercises, solitary meditation, engrossed socializing and also in all kinds of communal politics.

For over a decade my games teacher has insisted that I warm up and do my stretches before playing and I have never done it. I have even torn my hamstring as a result of jumping into a football game after a long bout of inactivity after which I have never been able to play the sport again. But just observe the Flamingos at dawn just before they begin their day. Each one will indulge in its own full body stretches, which will include leg and wing extensions, neck stretching in every direction and rotations, forward bends and a range of other warm up exercises which I am yet to find the right terminology for.

The foraging style adopted by a Flamingo hardly involves a patient gaze or a swift and accurate thrust like members of the heron or egret clan. Unlike them, its bill is a custom made implement for sifting through the bottom sludge for small grubs and drifting vegetation below the water. So it goes about employing it by plunging its head upside down into the water and sieving the mud for food. Intermittently it pulls out for a snatch of breath and then plunges in again. In deeper waters it simultaneously pedals the mud with both its feet, like working out on an Orbitrek, to uncover its hiding grubs. In more shallower and slushy areas, the bird walks around briskly swinging its submerged neck back and forth in long arcs. Social birds with a short temper, swinging about their heads haphazardly in search of food quite often ends in a breach of another's territory, or worse, "Bang" a collision. Either way, a brief melee ensues which involves the two Flamingos audibly snapping their bills and attempting to bite each other's necks. They quickly gauge one another's strengths and most fights last barely few moments. At the end, the frailer bird saves its dignity by making a hasty retreat to more peaceful waters, before being caught rudely by the neck and shoved away.

Seeing these petty conflicts, I can't help but feel that the Flamingos can learn a thing or two by watching the Spoonbills, whom they often coexist with within wetlands. The two have a number of common traits as in being social creatures and having an unusual bill, but most importantly a very similar haphazard swing-neck foraging style. Infact a Spoonbill goes forth in a more frenzied fashion such that Stilts, Stints and other small waders fly away from the vicinity to avoid being whacked. The bird is also always accompanied by a larger wader like a Great egret or a Swamp Hen closely at its side, which pick away the fleeing grubs it has flushed out or missed. But when hunting together a Spoonbill flock's movements are fairly orchestrated so that they not only avoid banging one another but the troop also seems to move forward in tactical formation.

The drab grey and black, juvenile flamingos stand like dirty blemishes near a brilliantly pink flock. Their foraging skills too aren't on par with the adults and are discernibly clumsy with their limbs. So to make matters easier, the younger ones are stringently excluded from the feeding grounds of the rest of the flock. Instead they are left to themselves, scattered over the wetland in less fertile waters where they hone their skills so that they can be inducted soon into the adult troop. Moreover, if a junior is lucky to find a good enough spot, a bullying adult may catch a glimpse of this and oust it from its location by force and occupy the place for itself. An under fed adult flamingo too lacks color, and you will find many such large lack luster ones at the start of the season.

At Chennai I normally go to the Pallikaranai marsh or the Perumbakkam wetland to watch Flamingos. It's usually after the monsoons that they gather at these places, but these birds are more nomads than they are migrants and their wanderings depend on water availability. After the floods of 2015 December, these birds were seen in the city during all subsequent twelve months of the year. This year however, after the rains have largely failed, the birds are already low in numbers by the end of January. Wetlands are rain fed and their water levels ergo variable. And Flamingos are very choosy about the depth they wade in. A surplus of water too they find uninviting. They usually like the waters to be somewhere between their ankle and knees, for only then are they able to scour for their food with ease. So in my wanderings in search of these birds in and around the city, I find that sometimes the best place to find them is in the backwaters of the sea. Along the East Coast Road there are many serene locations, some quite interior from the coast, where one can see these birds gather in considerable numbers. Last October I was on a birding trip with a senior friend and a fellow birder along the East Coast Road when we discovered that the Mudaliarkuppam backwaters had a high tide and hence had barely any birds in it. Having driven so far and determined to find more birds we diverted into a coastal village with the hopes of discovering a new birding site. On driving into a bridge under construction we saw, in a large inlet of the sea into a scrubland,specks of shimmering pink in the distance. We spared not a single local for getting the directions to the spot. We made it very clear that we were looking for tall, pink birds with long legs and beaks, which bought us many puzzled looks from lungi clad men who were all headed behind the bushes for the morning. Our search ended in success albeit after navigating unnavigable mud roads and through Eucalyptus plantations. Quite surprisingly this water body was right adjacent to a few cents of farmland, one being ploughed while in another about a hundred women were planting fresh paddy saplings. The birds didn't seem to mind the chatter of the crowd of ladies planting the rice. I got on all fours and crawled along the last levee's edge for a closer shot. The farmer who happened to be overseeing the planting took a while to grasp what the two of us were up to, sneaking about in his land. In a very amiable voice, he then shouted out to me saying that I could walk upright and normally upto the water's edge without scaring the birds as they were very much used to the presence of people. The birds were foraging only about forty feet away. Even then, few cared to even pull their heads out of the water to keep an eye on us strangers who were pointing long bulky black accoutrements at them. Anywhere else when I had tried creeping up so near to these birds, they would all stop dead and give me a grave stare with their heads held high. And then one bird, usually at one end of the troop will cautiously spread its wings and give a flap. That would be the signal for the entire lot to fly. The rest of the flock too would flap in agreement and then whole flock would relocate to a more secluded place. Instead here was a small but impressive scenario wherein the birds trusted us humans, when we have let them be and have passively coexisted with them. A dozen Golden plovers too, further ahead along the waterline didn't mind us too much and went about their business undisturbed. But as it often occurs, when things were beginning to get too good, there appeared a Marsh harrier from further inland, quartering close to the water, sending every last flamingo, duck and plover fleeing beyond our sight.

SOME ATTRIBUTES
OF A RAT SNAKE

ONE EARLY EVENING JUST BEFORE SCHOOL HAD reopened my colleague and I sat in the common room of our dormitory and were playing chess. It was after a long day spent in shifting cots and mattresses and getting all the dorms ready for use before the children arrived. We heard a hesitant knock on the door. On the first occasion we exchanged glances and nonverbally attributed it to the wind. Then there was a sharp metallic clang of the door latch outside being shoved to one side and then there were some more subdued thuds following it. My colleague got up to open the door. He even happened to yell out an affirmation assuming there was a person outside. But the knocks were not very confident ones. They were more like blunt nudges on the door and hence raised my suspicions. When my friend moved the latch and opened the door, he got a scare of his life. He was a man who was already petrified of snakes and when he pulled the door, the full length of a gigantic Rat snake, over seven feet long, fell over him, on his shoulder, chest and all. It had made its way up the door and was leaning on it near vertically before losing its hold and collapsing forwards. And as my colleague frantically darted back into the courtyard, into a clump of Aloe vera, the snake loudly threw itself around, jumped all the stairs and fled into the grass. The snake, I am guessing, took the support of the door to reach up near the solar light at the threshold, to catch that fat senile gecko which has been living under it for ages. Or it could have been after the winged termites swarming around the light. The gecko itself had gone pale and had hid squarely between the light and wall, with its limbs close to its body, least bothered of the plenitude of insects around. It had certainly caught a glimpse of the mammoth snake and probably just had a close escape. My colleague on the other hand was shuddering under his sheets all night to rid his mind off the unpleasant encounter.

The campus had many Rat snakes but this one was senior to them all. One of the farming staff told me that it had been roaming here for many years even before Pathashaala had started. It had an unmistakable steel gray skin whose silhouette would look jet black from a distance. When it crossed any of the roads, its body would cover the entire breadth of it and this is how many of us would describe this creature. Yet even for its great size, it would move so swiftly and could leap forward if it wanted to, leaving behind long diagonal tracks on the gravel. If it was on the Neem tree near our dorm, multiple garden lizards would jump off from its branches, fall on the ground and run in all directions. I have been lucky to see this snake in one or two of its combat dances with other males. I rely on the lapwings to spot a Rat snake combat dance for me. A passing snake is quite often enough to arouse these birds and two large Rat snakes vigorously wrapping and twirling around each other, send the birds into frenzy. They will circle and screech above the reptiles till the spectacle is over and the snakes glide out of their territories. I have seen smaller males struggle to tackle the weight of this large gray brute while they are constantly pinned down by it. The fights don't last long with this one.

Earlier during the holidays, I was called one morning to the dorm opposite mine as this Rat snake had entered the bathroom. Renovation work was going on inside and the floor was being relaid. Some of the workers had nudged the reptile with their crowbars in an attempt to move it out and the snake was left bruised on its flanks and on its back. Its temper had shot up to the peak and it pounced like a giant spring on anyone who entered the bathroom. Its each breath made its whole body expand and contract. It was now growling like a threatened Wolf and the sound resonated throughout the dormitory. No worker now dared to go near the bathroom. It spat out a mutilated Tree frog on my shorts the first thing, as if it threatened me of a similar consequence, when I entered the bathroom to remove it. I was armed with a dustbin lid to block its lunges. On picking it up and supporting and stroking its belly, its anger piped down. I would like to think or it felt like the snake recognized me, my smell, my shape or just my presence. We had run into eachother on so many instances over the years, seen each other in the eye so many times. Its body tied both my hands like a thick gentle rope as I carried it out which then unwound itself as the snake glissaded into the paddy field outside the dorm.

I wish I could call this snake species by some other name. 'Rat snake' speaks nothing of its allure or charismatic presence in the serpent tribe. Not of its large sentient eyes, or its agility or its coy. Moreover the creature has a catholic diet encompassing much more than rats. But it takes a snake of its speed to pursue and take down a rodent in the labyrinth of a Corn cultivation or a paddy field. A Rat snake is also an extremely alert animal. Its eyes are brilliant and so is its faculty to sense ground borne vibrations. If you came across a snake like a Checkered Keelback when it is eating a frog, it wouldn't care if you stood by it or sat next to it. It would solely be interested in its food. Only after moving its prey fully down its throat will it recognize you as a potential threat to itself and attempt moving away half heartedly. But if it so happened to be a Rat snake, it would sense you coming from twenty or thirty feet away and will lift itself a full metre off the ground to confirm its hunch. It would then observe you with a resolute gaze. Now if you so much as turned in its direction, whether you notice its presence or not, even if it had three quarters of a frog in its mouth, it would barf it out without a second thought and zip away.

Among all snakes, the juveniles are far more hot tempered than the adults. And this phenomenon couldn't be more pronounced than in Rat snakes. It is an easy task to lead an Adult Rat snake out if it has entered any of our spaces. Most often, once it knows it has been spotted it gets very nervous and will rush to the closest exit by itself. A small one however needs to be given a wide berth, otherwise it gets cranky. Move too near it and it will flatten its neck lengthwise and start rasping. And after that it will lose all intentions to head out and will try to nail whatever animate or inanimate touches it or nears it. Among my biggest misadventures yet, I owe to a juvenile Rat snake. This was when I was still doing my A levels at Pathashaala. One afternoon, just before lunch A Rat snake, hardly two feet long, had entered the classroom courtyard. I picked it up and showed it to some of the teachers in the staffroom and then left it outside. It was all purely for bravado, especially since it was a bunch of newly joined teachers inside. And then a few more teachers came along. I went out and found the snake again and brought it back to show them as well. The snake decided not to entertain this now for the second time. It flattened its throat and wriggled from side to side with a wide open mouth, indicating that it was losing its cool. It then abruptly turned around and clamped its jaws firmly onto my wrist. To make things worse, after I let go of the snake, I found that all the other teachers were narrating the whole story to a senior teacher who had just walked in. The drops of blood on the floor made her get more serious. I was at once put on a car with an accompanying staff and sent to the Chengalpet Government Hospital by the Head master. I begged to be let go and pleaded that Rat snake bites were as good as thorn pricks. I was given some Kalmegh leaves to chew instead. The queue to the doctor's room at the outpatient ward was a very lengthy one. My companion however told the person at the head of the line that I had suffered a snake bite and that it was serious. I was let in immediately. The doctor rose from his chair when he was told that I had a snakebite and asked me to be admitted immediately and have a blood test done at once. I begged again for some sympathy from him and told him it was a Rat snake. That seemed all the same to him. Then in a fit of desperation I asked the doctor whether he knew anything about snakes at all. The man got seriously offended and asked my companion whether the boy takes him for a doctor or a snake charmer and whether I was in my right mind. We were asked to wait outside but he didn't have the intention of seeing me again. School however insisted that I should get admitted since if anything happened then it would be held accountable. We waited for four hours after which the doctor's shift ended and his son took his place. To him I presented no arguments and readily got admitted in the casualty ward to prevent any further scene. By then news had gone to my mother who was in Chennai and she travelled all the way and arrived at the hospital utterly in panic. I was kept in the hospital till midnight and then discharged after exhibiting no symptoms of envenomation. It was among my most guilt ridden days. The very next thing I got was a grim firing from the school's Director over the phone. I have been cautious with cranky juvenile snakes ever since.

On the move, Cobras and Rat snakes may look very similar and it is important to be able to tell between the two, for our own sake and for the snake's. If the former spreads its hood then it saves you the effort. If not the best pointer to tell them apart at a glance are the black streaks running across the mouth of a Rat snake, from the upper lip to the lower lip, from one end to the other, giving its mouth a rugged look. But if you saw only the latter half of a large brownish snake is best to keep your distance. When I was still doing my high schooling at Pathashaala, I was summoned by the art teacher who wanted me to attend to a snake that had gone under a pile of gunny sacks he had stacked up for his mural work. Removing one sack after another I had finally exposed the snake's long tail. Now Rat snakes were an everyday sight here and there was no reason for this not to be one. So I grabbed it by the tail and pulled it out. Then out spread a wide hood within foot of my chest. Before the Cobra could decide upon any subsequent course of action I flung it into the vegetation. My lesson was clear. Don't judge a snake by its tail!

ANOTHER SKETCH OF A ROLLER

I HOLD VIVID MEMORIES OF THE INDIAN ROLLER from my childhood or I think even from late infancy. On long cumbersome car journeys in the dry brown and brazen heat of our country highways, on journeys I was thrown into and hence those I despised and wanted to run away from, the striking colors of a flying roller would lift my spirits, soothe my tantrums and displeasure for a while and would keep my face pressed hard to the window glass. Where did such ambrosial colors come from in such an arid land? I would imagine the bird to be a messenger from the sky, the only other thing nearly of the same complexion as itself. As the bird descended and alighted on a telegraph wire, I remember a great feeling of disbelief which overwhelmed me, as all the brilliant shades of navy and azure blue, abruptly vanished into its folding wings and leaving the bird now drab and dull as if its plumage had dissolved back into the skies. The bird's color and sudden lack of it struck me with equal fascination. After the monsoon rains the Roller's colors would evoke a different feeling of beauty against the dull skies, the chill air and the fresh wet verdure.

Westerners, when they first sighted the Roller in our country during their colonial wanderings, saw the bird and called it a Blue Jay, a bird of the North American woods. But just consider the breath taking resplendence of the Roller, oh the dazzling alternations of blue with every wing beat, does its Western counterpart even qualify for a comparison?

As a young boy, finding a roller's feather would amount to stumbling upon treasure, an exquisite gem stone. I would pick it up and keep it in my bureau and then hold it and twirl it between my fingers everyday to admire its colors once more. I would show it to my guests and my cousins when they came home. The feather would be a bookmark for my favourite book. Now much older, I see it where it is lying when I come across a roller's feather and cherish the memories it brings. And on nature walks I take children on, they too express the same wonder for it. All of them would keep a gimlet eye to be the first to find a roller's feather and take it back home. They would trade it, fight over it, wear it, or gift it to their dear ones.

Like a hermit in the hills, for most of the year the Roller is a silent and solitary bird. For much of the day it will sit still at its outpost, occasionally taking off and landing on an insect on the ground and then returning to its perch. It chooses its post, a high wire, a flag post or a tall stump, from where it can have a vast and unhindered view of the land and enjoys its feathers being ruffled by the afternoon wind. It picks no fights with its fellow birds and if a drongo or a crow challenged it over a territorial dispute, the Roller makes a silent and dignified relocation. Then suddenly, once in a few days, you will hear a choked guttural cough, a muffled sound yet one which echoes, and you will look around and wonder where on Earth the sound came from. You may even never figure out its source unless you see the Roller abruptly speak out in a fit of contemplation atop its wire. A call one wouldn't really call pleasant but one wouldn't mind either, because of its rare occurrence.

But by end of March, as the summer heat sets in, this bird is affected by the moods of romance. It renounces its silence and bursts into song with its bad voice. The male starts its courting display early in the day, flying to a high point and then looping in hysterical midair hyperbolas; a feat quite entertaining if they weren't accompanied by prolonged deep throated screeches, with accents and crescendos, like as if the devil himself was after it. This is the alter ego of the bird. The female scrutinizes from a distance I should assume. But which lady would be attracted to such maniacal demonstrations, like an ill omen and would want a man showing all the extreme symptoms of non compos mentis? I have come across Mynahs, Crows and other fellow birds sit by with a look of great revulsion, listening to a displaying Roller. After a point, when their thresholds of tolerance have spilled over, they fly up and chase the Roller out of earshot. You will especially feel grateful towards them for this action in case a Roller was going on and on right outside your room, even before you were out of bed. And may the Gods forbid the scenario of when two male rollers are displaying within each other's earshot. Each will scream louder and louder with each loop and will go on tirelessly attempting to outcompete each other.

There are a lot of classic descriptions by naturalists of the courting roller in the archives of Indian nature writing. Dewar, in his 'Bird calendar of Northern India' states, "… but none can be so deaf and blind as to miss the love making of the gorgeous roller. Has not everyone marveled at the hoarse cries and rasping screams which emanate from these birds as they fling themselves into the air and ascend and descend, as though they were tossed by unseen hands" Note that his tone is of sarcasm here because then he goes on to say "It is difficult to realize that the harsh and angry sounding cries of these birds denote, not rage, but joy." The legendary M.Krishnan in his essay, the March Roller, describes "… the courting roller goes plain crazy, abandons its perch and flies about with manic energy and aimlessness. It scours the heavens not in soaring circles, not in steep acrobatic loops, but just anyhow."

After nesting activities commence and the roller settles down to raise its brood, the land and its denizens greet the bird's return to sobriety. In the following months, the bird does however vocalize now and then but these are battle cries. Both rollers are protective parents and while the female is on the job of incubation, the male relentlessly deals with egg looters and nestling snatchers along with bringing food for its chicks. A tall palm trunk with a fallen off crown, either by a lightning strike or by old age, is very often chosen. The slight depression, right at the top makes an ideal place for a nest. I have spent a couple of months sometime back watching a pair of nesting Rollers atop a palm trunk at the edge of a village lake. The entire periphery of the lake was densely lined with Palmyras and in some places there was barely enough space between them to wedge yourself through. The hollows and fronds of the trees were homes to numerous Parakeets, Wood Swallows, Palm Swifts and Spotted owlets. With the other birds the parent rollers coexisted peacefully even if they perched on the very trunk the nest was on. They didn't mind the Squirrels either or the Garden lizards. But with the Spotted Owlets they were constantly at war. Now I haven't seen Owlets lifting nestlings so I don't know the entire premise for the hostility between the two birds. The owlets lived in little fist sized hollows on nearby palms. Nearly each morning, even before an owlet bobbed its head outside its hole, the male roller would fly back and forth outside rasping loudly, till the bird of prey jumped out, uttering equally unsettling cries, and flew away to a more silent edge of the lake. The roller would give it a short chase too at times. I think some of the owlets soon relocated to hollows far away from the roller's residence on being subjected to this daily harassment. Strong measures are taken against Shikras and Crows as well which knowingly or unknowingly perch close to the premises. And exactly once I have seen this pair give a ferocious chase to a Red-Necked Falcon.

After the demands of its family are met and its progeny is successfully raised, the Roller returns to its saintly existence. Its presence is now hardly felt. It now purely bears witness to what goes on around without mingling, without mixing, like a water drop on a lotus petal. And just as it is initially difficult to comprehend its vanishing colors as it perches, it is difficult to believe that this bird once for entire months made the loudest din in the land.

THE THRUSH AND THE PITTA

THE SECOND TERM OF SCHOOL IS ALWAYS AN exciting time and a period with least tension. Firstly there would be no reports given at the end of the term so one didn't need to keep a hard check on one's behavior. Moreover I had the privilege of going unrecorded if I did badly in any of the final tests. The School, KFI reopened by the end of September and most of all, at this time of the year, the campus would have many migrant visitors. It was a forested haven in the middle of Chennai city's din and for the birds it was an oasis. Warblers darted about in every bush. I never took up the tedium of properly identifying Warblers and gave them a different name each day choosing from numerous similar specimens from my bird guide. Each morning, all along the walkway from the car park to the games field, as people started arriving, the song and screech of the Golden oriole would be audible overhead and a few students and teachers would gather under a tree to spot it. On less frequented pathways near the principal's quarters, Forest wagtails would loiter about very earnestly shaking their behinds, briefly clearing the path and then returning, when someone came that way.

The arrivals I most eagerly awaited for were the Indian Pitta and the Orange headed thrush. These birds like their privacy very much and settle in the more silent and secluded spots in the campus. During school hours one hardly sees them but in the late afternoons when all the students and most of the staff have gone home, the birds begin to scout into every part of the school. I was picked up from school with a consistent lack of punctuality for several years. Not that I complained of it anytime. I had the daily opportunity to wander around in a large campus, not just on trodden paths but also around the staff quarters, near the school pond or even climb the huge Banyan tree (The School has the second largest Banyan tree in the city) all of which were prohibited places for students. But I could risk it as there were very few supervising eyes around at this time. But occasionally a teacher heading home late, would catch me trespassing and give it to me good and I would have to spend the next morning in the Principal's office. At times I would take a friend along with me against his will, but I would convince him by promising to show him a snake or something rare and the poor fellow would be in trouble too.

Hindsight reveals to me that it was on very few instances that I actually sought out the Pitta and the Thrush on my walks and found them. Instead what would usually occur was that I would go sit in a remote, wooded place out of sight from prying eyes and slip into reveries, those which would reveal themselves only in complete seclusion. Snap-snap...snap-snap-snap. Eventually the soft crackling of leaf litter would be heard and at the corner of my eye I would spot a Pitta or a Thrush come hopping on the ground, stopping to look under some dead leaves and then hop along again.

And if one sat very still, these otherwise secretive birds would hop a bit closer and give you deeply scrutinizing looks with every tilt of the head possible. Next they would hop over to the other side and study you from a different angle and then hop away and resume their foraging. This way I quite frequently came across these two birds. I would like to think that at heart, I was very much like these birds by nature, as a boy; I loved spending time alone in a secluded place in the shade and that's probably why I bumped into them so often.

While we look upward and crick our necks to spot other birds, to watch the Pitta and the Orange headed thrush its best to squat low in the undergrowth. The niche of both is strictly terra firma. They are similar in their feeding habits too and can regularly be spotted together. While the thrush is timid and diffident in its looks and manners, the Pitta is a trifle more bossy over its companion. It is not often happy sharing its space and drives the thrush away by charging at it if the latter gets too close to it or if it settled on any of its favorite foraging spots. The Pitta flaunts on itself every color one can find in an average pastel box but yet it is seldom satisfied with the way it looks. So every now and then it gives itself a meticulous preening, making sure it puts all the brighter feathers over the drabber ones. And it takes a bath several times a day in the cement water basin in which water would be filled for the school cows to drink from, avoiding the swings of the bullock's tail.

The name 'Pitta' comes from the Telugu word which simply translates into 'bird.' I had a firsthand discovery of its etymology before coming across it in any book. I had gone camping on a school trip to the Venkateshwara National Park in Mamandur, Andhra Pradesh. The native Shikari who accompanied us on our walks into the forest spoke purely Telugu and not an alphabet of English or Tamil. So both of us often ended up communicating in dramatic gestures and signs. Every time I heard a new birdcall coming from a Bamboo clump or atop a tree, I would ask the man what it was and he would instantly reply saying 'Pitta.' At the beginning I thought that the forest was teaming with Pittas, although I didn't spot any nor did I recognize all its new calls, but soon I began to have doubts when the bird's inventory of calls began to expand more and more. I fully realized the generic nature of the term he was using when he pointed at a Fantail which landed in front of us and called it a 'Pitta.' I am almost sure that the common name of the actual Pitta was born when some British officer posted in a rural corner of Andhra Pradesh, pointed at the bird and asked a passing local what on earth it was called. And the local with a confounded expression, in his native tongue would have told him 'well ofcourse it is a bird!'.

One of the Tamil names of the Indian Pitta, Aarumani-kuruvi, which translates to '6 'o' clock bird,' is more descriptive of its habits. An opera singer would describe the Pitta's call as a short messa-di -voce of four notes, the first two on a crescendo and the next two descending, all in immediate succession. What is most known of its call is that it only sounds it at twilight hours and in most places it is renowned to be punctual to the minute so much so that you can rely on it as your alarm bell.

In the Orange headed Thrush's repertoire there are several more notes and true to the name 'Thrush' its song is highly impromptu. And even the pitch and tone of these birds in different localities can be so varied that even a seasoned birdwatcher may want to see the Thrush before attributing it to the song being heard. Whether it's a misty morning or a scorching afternoon the bird doesn't take into account and seems to sing whenever it pleases, with its head held high and chest puffed out. Recently I read about the Indonesian National Songbird Contest held every year. The Orange headed thrushes are among the star contestants each year along with our very own White-Rumped Shamas, Blue-Winged Leafbirds and Magpie robins. These birds are much in demand to be procured and trained for this contest by virtue of their vocal gifts. They are judged based on three main criteria, namely song continuity, volume and repertoire. And in the year 2005 one Orange headed thrush was declared the winner of all three. It was described as a bird with extraordinary vocal power and stamina. Apart from the prize money, the owner was offered 250 million Indonesian Rupiah in exchange for the bird, but it was reported that he had declined it and instead chose to keep the Thrush he had known and lived with for five years.

In more wetter and forested places in our country lives the cyanotus race of the Orange headed thrush. Unlike its sibling, this is a resident bird and instead of a full orange head, it wears white eye patches which are grazed over by two thuggish black bars; markings better suited for its covert operations in places teaming with competitors and predators. Its voice is different too, being less resonant and shrill like a magpie robin's. I have noted that this bird seems less shy of people than its migratory counterpart for it lives with us throughout the year. It is fond of dropping in near camp sites, waiting by the roadsides to dine on crossing ant files and surreptitiously trailing trekkers up a hill and catching all the insects they flush along the way.

EGGLAY DELAY

SOME EARLY MONSOON SHOWERS CAN BE expected in August and September. It is then that many familiar faces which had withered away in summer after leaving behind their seeds, start to sprout again. Among them, the Passion vine (Passiflora foetida) is a tenacious creeper having heart shaped leaves and all the zeal required for survival. Fallow croplands thickly overgrow with Cyperus grasses along with Marsh Barbels and Pith plants. The Passion Vine always manages to find a wee gap in the vegetation to shoot forth one of its probing extremities. In a few days it would have risen up and spread radially over the grass tops, softly bouncing up and down on the undergrowth when the wind blows, like it were a trampoline bed. Near fences the springy tendrils extending from the Vine's stem, loop around the steel links like lassoes and climb up, over, down and beyond. Don't walk past a Passion Vine (or any other plant for that matter) without acknowledging its presence. They are beings with souls and a larger awareness and intelligence outside of thoughts and words. They have their own sentience. Notice that a Vine growing near a wall or a fence would grow a number of tendrils when it is several feet away, preparing itself to climb up well in advance while a prostrately growing one doesn't care to do so.

The flower of this creeper has a strong intoxicating scent, even mildly addictive I would say that I feel like bending down and sniffing them each time I pass by the Vine. Imagine how strongly it would seduce little insects which happen to be flying by or scurrying under, and then suddenly have their senses flooded by some strange fragrance. Ants and Bees gather at the nectarine moat around the flower's stamens and pistil, like animals coming to a waterhole. When its orange cherry sized fruits appear you will find their flat black seeds spat out in the corners of all the classrooms and under the tables. I give my class firm instructions not to walk through the undergrowth and pluck the fruits and time and again have confiscated many pocketfuls. But occasionally my students catch me shamelessly scouring a Passion Vine and collecting its fruits, having come to the classroom block early from breakfast.

But more than anything else this creeper is the principal host plant for the Tawny Coster butterfly's spiny red caterpillars. As the plants proliferate across the land the butterflies too begin to seek out mates and court them.

Unchivalrous advances by the male trying to forcibly impose itself on the female are predispositions by no means limited to just our own species. Among butterflies infact these acts can have the same magnitude of animosity, the most brutal one being 'pupal rape' wherein the cover of the pupa just beneath the abdomen of the female is broken by an avaricious male following which it copulates without having gone through the tedium of courting it. How does karma work for these insects I seriously wonder? Or am I always looking at these events with my dark polarizing anthropoid glasses? More common are the occasions when the male butterfly takes advantage when the female has just emerged from chrysalis and is yet to be able to move around or fly. With the Tawny Coster I have noted another habit of the same nature which I shouldn't be surprised if it was practiced in other common species as well. I well remember the very first time I noticed this several years back. I was on the way back to my dorm after a long day of teaching to change into sports clothing for the games period when I stopped at the road side, like a desert traveler having found a buried bottle of water, to gaze at a clump of Tridax flowers overflowing with butterflies. But like an unwelcome frog hiding inside the bottle, there came a male Tawny Coster fluttering by my side towards the flowers. Instead of seeking a vacant flower, it was suspiciously gaining height over the other butterflies and hovering like a hungry hawk above. Abruptly then, it dropped flat on a female Tawny Coster which was peacefully perched on a flower and pinned it to the ground, over the hot gravel on the road. Now desperately curling its abdomen, the male tried to force itself onto it. I think the scorching heat below made the female wrestle hard and quickly throw off its aggressor and then deftly fly to its escape. The struggle had left behind some of their orange and black scales stuck dry on to the little stones.

It is a subliminal experience to watch a female butterfly seeking out a leaf and then laying its eggs.

Probably because it is the first event which unravels into the greatest transformations one may witness on this Earth, so common place yet so miraculous. Probably because it has fed so much poetry and hope. Probably because it ineffably exemplifies the immense network of life in which the plant, the butterfly and I, come together for a while.

On the way back to Pathashaala after a survey activity in the nearby village, four senior students and I stopped by a large growth of Passion Vine by the campus fence. Some Tawny Coster butterflies were fluttering around over the vegetation. Calling the attention of my exhausted comrades who were greatly eager to have lunch, I promised them that they could see a butterfly laying its eggs if they waited for a while patiently. One of the four politely communicated his disinterest and left for the dining hall expressing that he would like to have his meals hot. To the other three, I pointed to a female Tawny Coster fluttering very close to the Passion vine and claimed, with a tone of certainty that it was shortly going to lay its eggs. Two of them simultaneously questioned me of how I knew this. I presented my arguments. Firstly it was a female butterfly. Secondly it had an abdominal cap and a notably bulged abdomen, indicating that it was bearing fully developed eggs. Next it was hovering around and periodically perching on its favored host plant. And finally it was the preferred part of the day for the butterfly. My comrades seemed rather impressed with my explanations and were willing to let lunch wait a while to watch this butterfly.

The butterfly would sustain our hopes by perching on a leaf after much fluttering around, and will slowly begin to pivot itself to the undersurface of the leaf and start bending its abdomen towards it. And as we watched open mouthed, anticipating the eggs to be laid at last, just then, to our acute frustration, a swift draught of breeze will blow away the butterfly. And then for the next several minutes the insect would flit all over the vine again, examining and bumping into many leaves before settling on a satisfactory one. The wind will blow again. This exasperating cycle repeated itself some half a dozen times and it had become half past lunch time. By now, the strong pangs of hunger and the prolonged futile wait had made one of my comrades furious with this whole affair and he refused to further comply with my requests to wait and watch the exquisite sight. Due to reasons of my answerability to school and also mild hunger, I submitted to his demands and joined my group to the dining hall before the butterfly managed to finally lay its eggs. On every subsequent occasion when I pointed out a prospective egg laying butterfly or if I even spoke of this topic, this particular boy would either raise a strong voice of discouragement or instantly vacate the premises to avoid being invited.

A female Tawny Coster is duller and more ground colored as compared to the bright orange male and it seeks out certain conditions to lay its eggs. Around noon is the best time to catch it doing so, the most sunny and windy part of the day. Unlike most other butterflies this one lays its eggs in large clumps, usually around fifty to eighty eggs, as counted by my students, on the under surface of the leaf. During the times when it is blown away before it can finish laying, it may disperse its clutch over several leaves. I suppose it chooses such a part of the day so that the eggs stick quickly and well to the leaf by virtue of the heat and aeration available. An interested bunch of students and I have gone on egg finding hunts on our evening nature walks, wherein we locate as many Tawny Coster egg clutches as possible, count the number of eggs and also note down the location in which it was laid. We learnt that the butterflies almost all the time choose vines which are well exposed to the Sun and avoided those which were in the shadow of trees or buildings. Moreover we discovered that in the handful of clutches we found in the shade, the eggs rolled off the leaf easily while we turned over the leaf to count them. But the ones on leaves open to sunlight adhered far more strongly. This observation also seems instructive of as to why this species of butterfly prefers the afternoon to lay eggs. But this isn't a generic phenomenon. Other butterflies like Crows and Tigers wouldn't mind anytime of the day and lay their eggs as and when they feel their labor pains. Some others prefer the dawn. Most moths ofcourse lay their eggs at night.

With this knowledge now I have put down for myself some pointers to be able to pinpoint a Tawny Coster which is about to lay its eggs. It must be around noon time or atleast sufficiently sunny or windy. Next the butterfly must be fluttering about suspiciously close to its feeding plant (and ofcourse it must be a female).

Then it must have a bulged abdomen and a brownish cap on the tip. This butterfly is known to develop this cap after it has mated to prevent anymore pesky males making further attempts on it. So if you are able to note all these pointers then the butterfly has no other business there than to lay its eggs. But as you may have inferred, the butterfly is after all finding the right nursery for its progeny to grow in and is a singularly choosy creature which may inspect two dozen leaves before settling on one while also striving against winds. Hence wait, wait like K.Ramesh describes in his poem 'not like an impatient child waiting for his father to bring gifts but like the tall trees in silence at night waiting to face the sunrise,' as waiting is the act of witnessing life unfold beyond the constraints of one's will.

RATS AND LEARNED HELPLESSNESS

HOW MUCH OF OUR FATE DO WE THINK IS SET IN stone? How much do our circumstances define what we make of our lives? How much of our destiny can be molded and shaped by our will?

I was the dorm parent for the first batch of tenth graders who stayed back in Pathashaala during the summer vacations to write their board exams. They were a batch of two and we all stayed together in the same room. And to just say that they were mischievous would be a gross understatement. When a teacher's back was briefly turned, they would put away their books and immediately commence to play cricket with broomsticks and stones inside the classroom and manage to break a few light bulbs. Biscuits and other eatables would go missing in the kitchen stores. During breaks they would climb up the building roofs. And one of them shared his bed and sheets all night long with Don. I would get up in the middle of the night and yell at both of them, and only then would my dog feel like tucking away his tail and exiting the place. Otherwise they were very sweet children.

The toilets in our dormitory were serene spaces during the day. But since school was on vacation and there were barely any people staying on campus, these rooms would become the playhouse of Lesser Bandicoot Rats during the nights. One of my fellow companions would valiantly chase away the creatures in the space with a mop stick or a broom before using. But the other boy would scream an invective and would come running back if he ever came across a rodent.

When problem turned crisis, we had a dozen rat traps bought and set up in strategic places in the dorm. The rats were lured like thieves to gold, to the smelly coconut pieces and masala vadas we used as baits. When we heard the sharp snap of the trap's spring go off at night all three of us would jump out of bed and rush to the spot. Don would already be waiting beside the trap salivating eagerly. We would set the rodent free before him and he would immediately grab it in his jaws and trot away out of the dormitory to consume his meat in solitude.

This way we quickly managed to do away with most of the rats partying in the washrooms. Infact we caught all of them, except one. And this last one was a mysterious creature. We never managed to see it. But whenever it was caught in a trap we had set for it, the wood near the grill on the trap's roof would be gnawed away and the rat would be missing inside. Many of our traps were laid to waste by it this way, and we finally gave up on trying to catch this invincible creature. But now and then the soft screeching of the tiles or a thud on a bucket would remind us of its presence. But what it was, how it looked like, how only it managed to free itself time and again, we never got to know.

A few weeks passed by. My two companions had completed their exams successfully, bade all of us at school good bye and had gone home. The other teachers too shortly left for their holidays. I was alone again in the company of the trees, birds and the butterflies. Then during one witching hour as I stood by the dorm courtyard listening to the crickets, the enigmatic creature decided to reveal itself to me. There it was, creeping down the corridor, sniffing along the floor meticulously, as if it didn't want to miss even a single molecule of air. There it was, the sole survivor of its tribe. There it was, the being which remained elusive to even death's grasp. I silently switched on a solar lamp to have a better look at this animal. It heard me and froze in its tracks. It was an extraordinarily alert creature. Its ears and whiskers twitched to the softest breeze and the faintest rustle. Its toes carried it like they bore no weight at all. I watched it without taking a breath. The rat then turned in my direction and began to creep towards me as it sniffed along the wall. Its eyes were milky white, devoid of any pupils, filled with cataracts. It was a blind rat. And its blindness had extraordinarily amplified the rest of its senses. I had to shuffle my feet only slightly for it to pick up the vibrations carried by the ground and discern my presence. Instantly it turned around and bolted away into the darkness.

I set a trap for it again that very night, not so much to catch it but to observe its methods. Then I lay sleeplessly shifting on my bed. I had just seen the creature I had hoped so long to get a glimpse of. This was no ordinary rat. It had survived to adulthood despite its great infirmity, in a land teaming with snakes, raptors, dogs, cats and mongooses.

When I heard the door of the trap snap shut I leaped and ran to it. The entrapped rat was scratching around inside the wooden box. It couldn't comprehend what it had run into. It only knew that it felt the cold air from above through the grills. Catching onto the metal grill with its tiny paws it gashed its incisors on the grainy wood edge of the roof with a frenzy to break free. In no time it chipped away enough of a gap, climbed out and on muffled feet thrust itself into the darkness again.

Why didn't the other rats do the same? Some of them were much bigger, brawnier, with front teeth like stone chisels. They could have cut through steel if they had wanted to. Why didn't they attempt to escape their death, the same way as their blind comrade?

Research by American psychologist Martin Seligman throws some light on the behavior of these rats. Taking Pavlov's methods a step forward, Seligman gave mild shocks to two groups of dogs which were free within a small barricaded space over which the dogs could jump over and escape from the discomfort. In the first group were dogs who were subjected to these shocks for several days while they were tied on a leash. So they couldn't escape their fate. The second group wasn't subjected to any shocks previously. When dogs from the second group were put in the enclosement and given a shock, they immediately jumped over the barricade and ran away from the hostile stimulus. The dogs from the first group, those who were already conditioned by the shocks, tolerated and accepted the maltreatment even though they had an opportunity to escape. They had "learned to remain helpless" and hence Seligman called this behavior learned helplessness. It is a strange case where existing knowledge curbs one from liberating oneself, where one accepts one's fate without questioning it.

So how much of our realities are we merely accepting as given without attempting to shape it and co-create it along with life. Another famous psychologist, Daniel Kahnemann, said the mind thinks that 'what it sees is what there is.' Can we actively push our perceptions to see realms beyond what is apparent, beyond what seems grossly real? Can we search for flood gates where we see full stops and discover that they exist?

So considering our friend, the blind rat who stalked the washrooms at night, its disability freed it from the conditioning the rest of its troop was under. It escaped because it couldn't see the trap! It escaped because it never knew it was trapped!

CALM AS A TOAD

KRRR..KRRRR..KRRR..KRRR..KRRR..KRRRR THAT familiar and deep throated grinding you hear all through a long monsoon night along with the other frogs and toads is the Common Indian Toad (Duttaphrynus melanostictus). The Burrowing frog screams out a precarious crescendo, as if it's throwing a tantrum, as if it has lost all its patience and is demanding a mate that very instant. The dilating and shrinking groans of a hundred thousand bullfrogs in the waterlogged fields stab into your temples and make you wonder if the building too is bobbing up and down. The toad on the other hand is tolerable, for its mating cries haven't in them too much fervor and lack any distinct character. I have even slept soundly during the times when one has crawled into my room. And after the nocturnal cacophonies die down, as the waters drain and dry, as the monsoon clouds get fully exhausted and tropical winter sets in, this toad's dispassionate call is still heard for several weeks more, now and then, here and there, in fits and starts, even after all its fellow amphibians have started burying themselves back into the ground to hibernate till the next monsoon. You may see them active even during the summer months of the year after some scant showers from the South west monsoons in June or July, whose moisture is barely sufficient to oust any to other amphibian.

All the walkways were once flanked on either side with head sized boulders at Pathashaala. And between their crevices were the mass abode of Common Indian Toads. Remove a rock or two and look beneath and you will find toads of every age group, side by side, one on another, sleeping and cuddled so closely that they may have made all the cracks watertight. One will also find them hidden beneath the low stone benches and they make good company on my solitary reveries in the evenings. They sometimes throw in a croak of affirmation when I have the right thought running in my head. All the toads wake up in unison and venture outside as dusk begins to settle. They are the second Anurans one most frequently runs into, the first place being taken by the pesky Common Tree Frogs. But in comparison to the latter, toads are far more polite and discreet in their manners. For starters they don't jump on your head or anywhere else from a window or a wall if they get frightened nor do they fall into dining vessels along with the tap water or clog wash basins by aestivating under the drains nor do they leave their frothy foam of spawn in drinking water cans. Worse is when an ill fated Tree Frog chooses to come and park itself right on the hinge of a door which is shortly going to be shut closed and then its skeleton remains stuck there for years to come. The toad however, likes the outdoors and remains firmly and thankfully on horizontal ground. If a passerby came along as it was crossing the road, it freezes, turns around and politely hops away in the other direction, leaving you your way. And if it knows that it is not in anyone's path, it remains cool and stays put where it is squatted. I have sometimes been fascinated by the way a toad gazes up at a solar lamp for considerable stretches of time and I have wondered whether the creature is in deep contemplation. Probably it is thinking how a star from the heavens is suddenly so close and so bright. Probably it is intrigued by the diffraction of light between its eyelids. Closer to the truth is that what it is really looking at with unblinking, unwavering eyes are the insects revolving around the solar lamp because as soon as a moth flies head on into the post, bumps on it and falls to the ground, the toad is quick to hop over and pick it off. On other evening walks I have seen them sitting by ant files, which are relocating to a different nest site because of recent rains. The toad will lift off one ant after another at its own leisure, while an endless number of these insects keep rolling by. I have observed only one exceptional event during when these toads awake and are active very early in the mornings and that is when winged termites take flight after the first rain showers and along with birds, spiders, bats and other predators, the toads too promptly join in the feast.

Monsoon morning…
the wing of a termite
on a toad's lip

On some weekends when I have had really nothing more engaging to do, I and a couple of my students with similar inclinations, have entertained ourselves by taking apart toad scats. These are large and oblong black masses and I must mention here that their owners have sometimes the uncanny tendency to relieve themselves perfectly in the middle of a road. A dried specimen when carefully taken apart can give valuable insights into the animal's dietary composition. Most of the insect carapaces are largely intact within them and an expert must be able to tell all the insect families it has eaten from recently, at a glance. I have occasionally chanced upon partially digested worm snakes and scorpion pincers in Common Indian Toad droppings, among other things. And more interestingly I have also occasionally chanced upon rubber bands and staple pins.

A full grown female toad is a gigantic creature and can be as large as a child's head. It is more upright than it is long, with a notable pot belly. Its skin over its back is packed with large dry black tipped warts, blotched with maroon and brown, like it has a layer of algal growth over it. Dark black ridges circle its lips and eyes, which appear like thick framed spectacles, giving it a serious and solemn look. When you catch one it may initially hang loose for a few moments but it will soon start scratching you with its hind legs. And you may want to hold its posterior away from yourself because if the toad is not able to free itself even then, it will exude a copious jet of urine on its handler as its next measure. And be sure to wash your hands immediately after, for you would have rubbed your fingers on its poison glands. Don, my companion dog, once grabbed a Common Indian Toad in his mouth (I was feeding him quite well) and was playing around with it by biting onto it and letting go. Soon his mouth got terribly swollen right upto his neck and he started to salivate profusely. After sprawling around on the ground in an uncoordinated state for half an hour or so, he got up and carried on with his life.

The male toad is puny and is about twenty times smaller than the female. It is hardly a few inches in any direction and its skin is much more delicate. It too has a baggy vocal sack beneath its mouth to sing with and impress a mate. The courting between the two is a rather amusing spectacle which invariably happens at my dorm's doorstep. The male after great efforts climbs over the female and tries to persuade it while the latter is always least interested. And it being several times stronger, kicks it away while it tries to get a grip on its back or throws on the ground and walks right over its face. Quite often many males try to climb on and pin down the female to make it spawn but, even three or four together still are no match for it.

A large female toad is really at the apex of its food chain where it lives but not because it's a top predator in any manner. Firstly many would be avoiding these toads because they are poisonous but still the juveniles and the males get often eaten by snakes, which show great immunity to their toxins. But a female toad is too big to fit into any snake's gob, even the one of a large Checkered Keelback. So if some small snake like a Striped Keelback gets overly ambitious and grabs it from behind, it simply fills its lungs, bloats up even more and then waits calmly. The snake will now strain to open its stretchy mouth wide enough to somehow fit this creature into its gullet, but the toad knows very well that there is no way on earth that this is going to happen. It has been through this drill so many times that it finds the ordeal more tedious than painful. The snake's teeth barely even puncture the toad's thick hide. And by the time the snake has even advanced its jaws a few millimeters up the body, you feel that its cheeks are going to tear apart and its eyeballs are going to fly out. It squirms its body and tries for a while more. Eventually it gives up and lets it go, and the toad hops away rather nonchalantly with its rugged head held high, leaving the snake heaving for breaths and adjusting back its overstretched jaw ligaments.

A BARBET'S HOLLOW

WHILE AT THE YUGAANTAR CONFERENCE AT THE Bhoomi College in Bangalore, I chanced upon a White cheeked Barbet's hollow. It required no keen eye or an arduous search to find it. There it was obviously, directly facing the walkway, some eight feet up the trunk of a Singapore cherry tree (Muntingia calabura), and right beside the entrance to the main building of the campus. Just beneath it, staff and students constantly fled in and out in preparation for the upcoming sessions of the event.

The hollow looked like it was a long cavity within the craggy tree trunk with a perfectly circular hole, as if it was stenciled out, for an entrance. There were two more hollows, abandoned albeit, just below this one at different angles and I wonder if the parent barbets ever were in the habit of raising two broods simultaneously. Now only this one, shown directly over the walkway, had chicks in it. From the squawks and squeaks I could hear as I stood below and strained my ears, I would say there were about three little birds inside the hollow. One of them perpetually peeped out its curious head and watched the world outside, leaving its siblings to quarrel beneath. Its bright pink flesh was seen between its sparsely growing neck feathers and its large eyes were all pupils, no white.As seen from a little hole up a tree, only a little bigger than an eye's orbit, the vast world outside must seem a strange and wondrous vista. I wonder what was kindled within the little bird's heart, to which this land is still foreign and nature still a mystery, as it watched the changing skies against the still trees or the incessant activity of the beetles and the bees around the summer blossoms of its tree.

During the breaks between sessions and during the free spaces in the evenings, I came to watch the Barbet chick, watching the world. The Singapore Cherry tree was bearing copious fruit. And even as Bulbuls, Orioles, Leafbirds and Koels indulged themselves day in and day out, there came about no dearth of the red berries, nor not anytime soon. Tiny flowerpeckers came to the remaining flowers on the canopy and perched upside down on them to draw in the nectar. The Barbet chick watched all this wide-eyed with its head tilted to one side, one eye facing the sky.

Over to one side of the tree was a well trimmed hedge, behind which I squatted to secretly observe the chick's behavior over the three days of the conference. Expressions of great dismay crossed their faces when a few of my distinguished colleagues spotted me squatting behind the vegetation in broad daylight and I had to reassure them of my intentions by pointing out to the tree and the nest.

As people went back and forth along the pathway, the young bird's head would follow their footsteps with an unblinking stare all through, right to the extent till which its stubby neck would allow from its hollow. It would try to follow the movements of squirrels running about, chasing eachother and squealing in spurts from the canopy. Once in a while a staff member would step out of the office to attend to a phone call. From above the young barbet would listen intently to the private conversation. If an eye at anytime happened to turn towards the nest, the overtly inquisitive bird would all of a sudden feel shy, drag back its head and slowly sink into its hole, keeping just one eye above it. Then later it would come out again when it feels it is not going to draw anyone's attention.

The parent White Cheeks would come intermittently to the hollow to feed the nestlings. At other times of the year, their sole activity the entire day would be to sit on a lofty branch and sound their repetitive calls, which soon becomes part of the background noise of the landscape. Breaks for fruit and nectar would be very short and they soon are back to their calling posts again. Whether the Rooster crows or the Robin sings or the Cricket chirps, the Barbets will shout. But now both the parent birds work overtime to raise their young and the land seems to have fallen unusually silent. They bring the chicks fruits from the same tree, the red berries and also green ones from the Hill Neems. They bring Katydids and Mantises from the organic fields around. Sometimes they excavate the leaf litter in the compost pit and bring back fat beetle larvae. And from the Litchi orchard nearby, they would bring strips of sour unripe litchi fruit.

The sibling which likes to peep out of the hollow, barricades the entrance and demands every feed for itself. Its beak which it holds wide ajar when a parent comes with food, fills the entire hole. It will clasp it then over the adult bird's beak till it lets go of the food into its mouth. The chicks below try to rise up to get their fair portion of the feed but are shoved down by the dominant sibling. But parent birds are parent birds and make sure that all their children are cared for. They push aside the snatching chick, when it has managed to already consume an extortionate quantity of the grubs and berries they bring, and squeeze themselves down into the nest to feed the rest of their progeny. But at some other times the chick above placidly gives them their way and continues to observe the happenings around it.

One day when it grows up and has to fend for itself and raise its own family, will it still find the leisure to watch the stars and the skies? Will it still find the time to be entertained by the strange activities of the human beings below?

But now it watched unwaveringly as the gardener carried the long hose pipe, much of it trailing behind him on the sand and then watched him water all the plants. It watched the yellow leaves spinning rapidly as they fell from a branch of the tree to the ground. It watched as I and everyone else bore our luggage and boarded vehicles and left to our homes.

There is only the act of watching, of being aware. Like the little barbet from its hollow. Our efforts and intentions are but the insignificant drifts and wiggles of brownian particles, our volition a sand grain in the tides. Does it matter to the Universe if we sink or float? Our legs kick back frantically and our hands grapple forward in this vast void of nothingness, of everythingness, but the enormity of existence keeps us tethered to our centres like little thumb pins, denying us any movement at all, letting life smoothen the ripples, correct its current and take its course anyways. Only the silence and surrender of awareness is real in the universal dance of this mind-body-space continuum.

ACQUAINTING WITH THE BRONZEBACK

I WAS CONDUCTING A CERTAIN SCIENCE workshop, as part of the outreach programme of Pathashaala, at the Aanoor village school. The presentation on the topic and an activity based on it were over and a slip test was going on in the compact classroom with narrow steel benches, where the students sat shoulder to shoulder. I was striding up and down the classroom attending to any clarifications which came up. Just as I was doing so, a sudden and horror laden uproar burst out in the neighboring classroom which made all of us jump in this one.

It sounded like a whole lot of people who were screaming for their lives. A few times I even heard names of some of the local deities being called upon. My colleagues and I ran to the spot prepared to meet a room full of students and teachers trapped in a fire, or some emergency of that sort. There in the classroom I saw no fire but here is a description of the scene which glared in front of us. At each corner of the classroom there were about five to six middle school children who were screaming in tears with expressions of utter horror. There was an even greater spectacle in the room which I wondered why it didn't strike me as the first thing there. On top of the table, not far from the entrance, was the teacher of the class clad in a glimmering sari, with her hands cupped over her ears as she screamed in spurts of hysteria. Her tear brimmed eyes were as wide as a squid's and they were transfixed at something on the floor. Also on the table were two girls hugging tightly onto the teacher with their faces buried in her sari. While this was happening a few boys came dashing to the door and ran out, shoving us out of the way. Apart from all this appalling drama the room looked quite normal and for several seconds I simply couldn't fathom what the cause of such a display of panic was.

I then tried to follow the gaze of the teacher. The floor before her elevated self was strewn with school bags, notebooks and pencil cases, in quite a disarray. For a second it was rather fantastic for me to think that the mess in front of her was the cause of her horror. But certainly it wasn't that and in a few moments the source of the pandemonium revealed itself from under a school bag.

A long slender neck at the end of which was a pointy head bearing large black eyes and a flicking tongue, peeped out from beneath the school bag. It seemed completely apathetic to the commotion it was causing around it. It was Mr. Bronzeback who had apparently entered the classroom through the open windows probably in pursuit of a gecko or a frog. Once the snake showed itself again, the amplitude of the vocalizations in the room rose once more. It was a full grown adult, over a metre long. I walked up to the snake. On my arrival the serpent slid around the bag and tried undulating itself on the smooth cement floor to the other end of the classroom, but I picked it up and let it curl around my hand. This action abruptly ended the racket. I walked out of the room to release the snake in some bush or thicket, responding with polite smiles to the requests, which became commands, of some of the teachers to kill the poor creature. The snake's blue tongue oscillated so rapidly that it was invisible until it became stationary. As I walked to the compound the snake now was probing its tail into my sleeve and then with the tip it managed to tickle my underarm. I unwound the creature and let it go in the grass on the other side of the school's compound.

On my return to the premises I received applause and appreciation. As a matter of fact my workshop was actually scheduled on the previous day but I had it postponed due to a knee injury. One teacher emphatically claimed that it was fate which had arranged these events so that I could come the next day and save the school from the terrible beast. I tried telling the teachers that this was a Bronzeback, a non-venomous snake and an utterly harmless one. But another teacher declared that all snakes were dangerous and intended harm to man. Just as playing darts cannot penetrate a brick wall, so could factual counter arguments not even graze the manifold myths which were prevalent about snakes.

Coming back to the Bronzeback, this snake too has an uncanny tendency to enter rooms or human inhabitations given the smallest gap or breach. It happens unfailingly every few days in the campus of Pathashaala. It has entered bathrooms (often not when in use), staff residences, dormitories, but most of all, the library (it is also an avid reader). It's a diurnal snake so anytime someone speaks or screams of a snake which has entered a building during the day, you can almost certainly call it off as a Bronzeback treesnake. I suppose the concrete indoors are cooler during the hot afternoons or probably it's the profuse house geckos and the invertebrates in our living spaces that the snake is after. Usually the Bronzeback is a leathery gray-black on the upper side and milky white underneath which is what you look for to spot it when it is on trees. Its large round black eyes are diagnostic and give it a look of inquisitiveness. When it is nervous or threatened the snake expands its scales on the upper half of its length to flash an iridescent blue beneath them and you will find it the most nervous thing, you have ever come across. During the times I have been called upon when this snake has entered a colleague's room, I often find the snake curled up on the top-most grills of the large windows, basking away. When I approach it, it gets so anxious that on many occasions it has jumped off the window right onto my face and musked on my nose. I also remember once when a student was walking to the games field she happened to pass under a low branch of a Neem tree on which again a Bronzeback happened to be on. The snake, in fright, fell off the branch squarely on her shoulders and from there leaped to the road's edge and bolted away. Notably, during another occasion on the same tree and possibly the same snake happened to be in pursuit of a Garden lizard just when a gang of boys were on their way to games. This time the lizard jumped off the tree and landed on one of them.

The elasticity this snake exhibits is astounding as well. On a few occasions when I was summoned to the common toilet, to remove a Bronzeback which had made its way in, the snake on seeing me would enter a wash basin filter, squeeze through the outlet pipe and escape. Once a Bronzeback entered the hollow space within the ceramic of the wash basin through the overflow hole and refused to come out no matter how much I shook or banged the porcelain. After removing the basin from the toilet, two boys and I kept the basin just outside the toilet and sat guard beside it, just to see the snake coming out. It was on a weekend and we waited from right after breakfast till lunch. We tapped and turned the thing over and over around but the creature just wouldn't come out. One boy lost his patience and all of a sudden lifted the porcelain piece and slammed it on the ground before I could even say Jack Robinson. I was contemplating about doing the same thing though but ofcourse I wouldn't have done it. The innards of the broken sink revealed no snake within it. Later the school plumber came along and educated us that the overflow hole of the sink has an outlet into the drain too and that the snake was never inside at all for all those hours.After lunch, all three of us were given a lengthy firing by the Director of the school for destroying school property.

The Bronzeback is also an excellent climber of trees and if needed, with remarkable speed, and can now and then be seen even jumping from one branch to another in pursuit of its prey. This attribute also makes the snake an egg-raider. Speaking of eggs and the Bronzeback I remember a nature walk, wherein a group of students and I observed an adult Bronzeback engrossed in making its way up a twenty foot Palm tree. At the other end, on the fronds of the Palm hung about half a dozen Baya weaver bird nests and the serpent's inclinations were certainly towards their eggs or the young fledglings. It was a thrilling sight to watch it climb. It made best efforts to make contact with the roughest parts of the bark to get enough traction to keep moving upwards but some parts of it body would slip off the trunk every few feet. Sometimes the snake would precariously slide down some distance but then would manage to get its grip again and persist to climb. At last when it was nearing the nests all the adult weavers settled on the crown of the Palm and started causing a loud commotion. The weavers which were nesting on nearby trees also joined in. Once the snake was within reach of the nests it lifted its neck off the tree trunk and inserted it into the closest nest while the rest of its body held unsteadily on the trunk. The racket of the birds grew louder. Some even hovered close to the snake and clawed it with their feet causing the reptile to wriggle its body away in order to avoid them. During these attacks the snake almost lost balance several times. At this point I think I had a strong hunch of how this whole episode was going to end. As the snake groped around in the nest with its head, out flew a female Baya from within the nest, which had probably been incubating her eggs inside and this threw the snake backwards. The Bronzeback started a free fall from all twenty feet and during its descent it frantically undulated its body as if it was swimming in water. Its fall ended on a thorny Prosopis bush beneath. All of us watching this scene thought that the creature had met its end impaled by the thorns. The snake hung loose from a branch for some time. But then it lifted itself, gave two curious looks hither and thither and casually glissaded through the thorn laden branches and made its way down the bush.

THE LIFE IN A PADDY FIELD

THERE HAVE BEEN TIMES WHEN I HAVE SAT ALONE and dreamt of living an agrarian life, not for anything else but for the closeness to Earth such a life offers. Not that my body is built for the arduous routines of farming. When the rice planting is happening at Pathashaala, on a few occasions, I, along with some students, have volunteered ourselves to also participate in it. We are given a contemptible corner of a field far from the main planting. The village women who come at daybreak to do the rice planting continue till the evening. But in my case within half an hour of bending my back about a hundred and fifty degrees from my hip girdle, I start noticing strong symptoms of vertigo and my backbone refuses to return to their original position for a long time. When not too many eyes are looking, I quietly walk out of the field like an Australopithecus. Some of the kids, who have been waiting for the chance to do the same, while also not wanting to be seen as the first person to leave the field, follow behind me.

The cultivation of paddy, right from sowing to harvest, is entwined with the livelihoods of all of our country wildlife. Many days before the planting, the acres weed laden fields are pumped with water with a five horsepower motor so that the hard baked ground becomes tender enough for ploughing. The ploughing tractor arrives one afternoon and I request the driver to allow me to sit beside him while the vehicle works on the fields. The sound of its engine is to birds, what the lunch bell is to the students. On certain occasions I have counted upto fifty Bee-eaters and Black drongos along with a few Kingfishers, Treepies and Flycatchers, congregate on the wires and trees nearby and almost the same number of Egrets and Pond herons gather on the levees and in the adjacent fields. Over the decades these birds have learnt to distinguish between the noise of this vehicle from all the others. A friend and fellow birdwatcher told me that in his village the tractor would at times be parked by the fields the previous day, since it comes from a distance, and he has observed birds camping overnight in the vicinity even before the machine got to work the next morning.

As the tractor's blades roll while it rattles up and down the field, it shreds through the overgrown vegetation like a giant horizontal mixer grinder. Centipedes and crickets are tossed up, spiders and rice field crabs scamper out of the way as they lose their cover and many more insects take to their wings to escape the annihilation. Cattle egrets and Pond herons follow closely behind the tractor, not caring about the slush being splashed on them, picking up all the maimed insects and crustaceans and their limbs, carapaces and entrails strewn along the way. Any lucky escapees too are confronted by a fleet of ravenous beaks. All the other birds which have gathered swoop down upon quarry left exposed on the water or catch them mid air as they flee. The greatest spectacle of all is the appearance of Whiskered Terns. One rarely sees them so much inland as they prefer hanging around near wetlands. But once the ploughing begins, I don't know who sends word to them, but sooner or later these Terns too turn up for the feast. They may even arrive only the next day to salvage the left over scraps, but they definitely do come each and every time. To croplands closer to the coast the larger Caspian and Gull-billed Terns also drop in at this event but only the Whiskered make it much further inland. Terns are the experts when it comes to catching waterborne prey and they don't bother getting their feathers and feet wet. So when they arrive on the scene, the Drongos and Bee-Eaters find them tough competition. Black Drongos however are vile creatures and will use thuggery to attain their ends. They sit waiting and plotting amongst themselves on the telegraph wires till a Tern swoops into the water and returns with a grub in its bill. Immediately two or more Drongos pounce at it screeching threateningly and lunge and harass it till the bird drops its catch and beats a frightened retreat. The paralyzed prey on the ground is then consumed by one of the ruffians and then they return to their perch, eagerly waiting till the next Tern rises with a catch.

More than a hundred women from the village come to the campus to transplant the rice saplings from the seed bed to the fields where they will grow till maturity. They are paid between a hundred and fifty to two hundred rupees for the day's planting (depending on area and duration of work) and some of my colleagues from the administration even skip their meals to supervise the planting. In a crowd like this it is very difficult to see who is working and who is just miming with the group and invariably each time a handful of ladies suddenly turn up on the scene just when the cash is being distributed, claiming their payment as well for the day's work.

The mass irrigation of the paddy lands stirs a whole community which has been dormant underground who otherwise wouldn't awake till the monsoons. Rice field crabs surface from their subterranean tunnels along with their co-hibernators, the Apple snails. So do many snakes. A host of frogs which were erstwhile practically fossilized within the rock solid sun-baked clay, soak up life from the moisture and emerge through the cracks. Soon butterflies like the Evening browns, Bush browns, many Skippers and a vast variety of moths flit about the rice plants, surveying for good spots to deliver their eggs. Some Erebid moths lay dozens of eggs on a single blade of rice and die right there post-partum still clutching on to the plant. Look for all their caterpillars hiding within the folds of the leaf sheaths and bored-in stems.

A paddy leaf is a lavish lunch table for many a spider, and hence they too are quick to immigrate into the new crop. Each time I take a walk on the levees, gazing across the cropland, I see several Wolf spiders or Lynx spiders with Asiatic Rice-borer moths between their mandibles, which are among the principal pests of paddy. Signature and Silver orb spiders build snares across saplings to trap airborne pests. Perenethis spider species surf on the water patrolling for prey near the stems. My partially identified photo-checklist of spiders

I have spotted in the paddyfields within the campus has about twenty five species in it. Surely these arachnids are the chief pest controllers for any crop. And to their ranks one must add the Water scorpions, the Dragonflies, Damselflies and their larvae swimming in the water. Birds like Prinias, Cisticolas and Warblers too do their part in insect and caterpillar control but they appear only after the plants have reasonably grown and their stalks are sturdy enough for them to perch on. One will find that an organic field is of immensely greater interest to the naturalist than a pesticide laden one, which is practically a green barren land with no prey, no predator, barely any life, hardly any drama.

Mr. Kanniappan, the late on-campus farmer, used to tell me that the Rice field crabs and the Apple snails are the unseen, unsung menaces to the rice crop. The crabs snip the tender parts of the sapling under the water with their pincers and consume the tasty bits. Especially a newly planted crop is a paradise for the crabs and a crab affected part of the crop has little shreds of rice sheaths floating on the water and the crop over time starts turning brown. Snipes arrive soon to put a check on these crab orgies. These birds wait patiently outside the tunnels of these crustaceans and use their long stocky bills like harpoon whalers to stab their quarry when they surface. An empty carapace and a pair of dismembered pincers wiped clean of their innards just outside a tunnel is a sure sign of a Snipe's presence. But even if the bird is unable to contain them, the local staff from the village frequently take home some crabs in little steel buckets to make a spicy gravy with them at home and have it with boiled rice.

Apple snails on the other hand are more secretive creatures. They are aquatic and host a dense carpet of algae on their shells which helps obscure them from view in the slush of the paddyfield. Just under its eyes are its several tentacles which it uses to execute swimming strokes and grope around for food. When it is disturbed, it has a trapdoor or an operculum attached to the end of its body using which it will shut tightly the shell's opening and stay indoors. My late friend told me that these creatures graze on the roots of the paddy and overtime make them wilt. So if he sees them when he is working on the field, he collects them and flings them one by one over the fence. Some of the locals, the youth especially, prefer having these snails roasted and salted along with their liquor. But he despises them all together. Nature has a custom designed control for these slimy Gastropods. It is more likely to find Open-Billed Storks in cultivations than in marshes or any other wetland habitat, quite possibly because its prey's preference for habitat is changing too. These Storks forage in flocks but not a single plant do they flatten as they stalk for snails. And I say so with certainty because these birds spend many hours every day in these fields for months together and if they were in the habit of treading on the rice plants, the whole crop should have been underwater within days. The adult birds have a gape caused by the downward curvature of their lower bills but this feature of its bill is not to use it like a nutcracker as is popularly theorized. To know this first hand, do examine a patch of a field attended by the Openbills. You will find that whole and unbroken empty snail shells are left behind by them. The only thing I have seen it use its gape for is to carry a snail it has found away from its snatching comrades, to relish it in privacy. The stork uses its bill instead to wedge its beak into the operculum of the slippery mollusk and on getting a grip at the creature inside, shakes the shell off and swallows the soft body. Often the bird is nimble enough to silently creep up behind a snail while it is moving around, with its body outside, and catch it before it tries to shut itself in. But for the larger part of the day, the Openbill storks spend their time lazing on bare canopies, with hunched backs and stretched wings, feeling the sun and the breeze, till their breeding duties begin and cut short their leisure.

The other reason I suppose paddyfields attract many water birds, barring its diversified range of prey supply, is that the irrigated water levels are just right for them to wade in and hence one can always find some waders here. Sandpipers, Stilts, Stints, Plovers and Shanks too use these fields as foraging grounds while they spend the winter in our country. The resident White breasted Waterhen is like Shakespeare's soldier, 'Jealous in honour, sudden and quick in quarrel' and walks about boisterously like a landlord who has let the rice cultivation on lease for all the other creatures. The Yellow and Pied wagtails though are content with whatever morsels they can find while they patrol up and down on the levees.

The whole landscape of our countryside transforms its complexion as the rice kernels mature. Like when the Oak forests enter autumn, our Paddyfields turn from a soothing, pacifying green to a gaudy golden shade which tickles the eye in the sun. Change also do the agrifauna as now the stalks of the rice plants have thickened and its panicles hang on every side with the weight of the grain, leaving little space in between them. Few waders can now be accommodated in the fields but the Waterhens and Crakes still skulk about in the grid of archways beneath the crop.

As the grains ripen more and more they require lesser water and one will stumble upon Rat snakes and Cobras frequently on the prowl which take down the Rats which are busy ransacking the grain. Flocks of Weaver birds, Tri-colored, Spotted and White-Rumped Munias too, make the most of all the fresh grain available before the harvest. I can't bail out these seed eaters in any way from all the plundering they do, quite to the acute exasperation of farmers. From what I have seen, much of a farmer's job on his fields during this part of the crop cycle is to run from one end to the other, yelling and chasing away troops of Weavers and Munias which have descended into his crop. But just as the river gives back to the ocean the moisture it constantly lends it, so too we owe Mother Nature a portion of our harvest so that she can continue to give, so that the cycle is completed. And these little seed-eaters are Earth's own agents. Let us bear in mind that apart from a handful of birds, the dozens of others which visit our fields are beneficial to the crop. It is land greedy Real estate and water greedy Soft drink factories which are the real savage threats to our farmers and our food production.

Harvest is a celebration for us as well as for all the life around. As the enormous harvesting vehicle clatters and chugs to and fro cutting the stalks of rice, the birds once again gather to feast on the fleeing invertebrates. When it leaves, the land is strewn with grain which is food to all the granivores which now can feed without being felons. On Pongal day the whole school gathers and we express our gratitude to earth for giving us our sustenance and eat the freshly harvested rice boiled in an earthen pot. There is a different quality of respect everyone feels when the rice one eats is part of one's landscape, part of one's life. The horns of the school cows are painted and are adorned with turmeric and saffron, honoring them for giving us our daily milk. Stumps of sugarcane are then eaten by everyone and the older boys rip the tough skin off the cane and give the juicy insides to the younger kids. And for the next few days endless ant files criss-cross the pathways, each ant carrying a single rice kernel in its jaws, back to its nest.

Harvest over…
ants enter their nests
with fresh grain

A BRIEF CALENDAR OF
BAYA WEAVERS

DECEMBER MORNING. MORE THAN THE COLD weather, the vapor rising from the boundless expanses of paddy cultivations would create the veil of winter mist in this part of the country. The trills of Sandpipers and the twitters of Yellow wagtails are the first sounds to emanate from these fields. And if one sat near the village lake during this time of the year one could actually lick the moisture off the air.

The flocks of Weaver birds also begin to swell just as the winter rice crops start to ripen. One wonders where such a large number of birds were hiding for all these months. Now and then I think I have seen a few along with the House sparrow troops raiding a rice mill. Or one or two of them one day abruptly on an electric wire. Yet it always occurs that one fine morning, in the middle of the month, as I take a walk down the campus road, I suddenly stumble upon row after row after row of telegraph wires, above the paddyfields, saturated with these birds. They wait on their perch, fidgeting like fifth graders, for the farmer below to walk over to the next field. Then immediately they plummet downwards in their hundreds and disappear into the blades of rice. Shortly the farmer would return after digging up a bund or switching on the water pump.

On noticing the peculiar quiver suddenly on all the plants of his crop, as if something was nudging them from the bottom, the annoyed man waves his sweaty towel about and shouts out madly. The weavers, then rise from this crop and flutter away in little parties to some other unattended field nearby. These drab gray congregations are always dotted here and there with deep red. Tri-colored Munias are always welcome into weaver flocks, whether it is the Baya weavers of the plains or the Streaked weavers of the Marshes and Reed beds. They are greeted and treated as their own. Furthermore it isn't uncommon to see a munia take up tenancy in an abandoned weaver nest alongside actual nest holders.

The Baya flocks have no dearth of feeding grounds in this countryside. Their mornings maybe spent in rice pastures, moving pickily from one field to the other, spoilt for choice. Following this a visit maybe made to a Peanut cultivation where they may feast on the multitude of menacing insects on the crop along with birds like Rosy starlings and Parakeets, the latter of whom I suspect have a greater taste for the nuts than the bugs. And then a little sortie maybe made to a hedge of Lantana for a snack of berries coupled with a drop in at a millet field or at a cowherd's backyard to raid the fodder corn he has stacked up for his cattle. Afternoons call for a siesta by the cool of inundated croplands or in the shade of Prosopis thorns. But soon they are on the lookout again for untended rice as this would be the best time of the day to plunder without any hassle. Be wary when you choose to take a walk on the narrow and slippery levees of rice cultivations to be lost in the verdure of a rustic landscape. The breezy silence will be suddenly broken by the tumult of a hundred wing beats rising from the crops. This is enough to knock off your balance and you, into the slush. These flocks can also be found on pastures, near grazing cattle, for whatever grub or grain is flushed by their hooves. Evenings culminate with the birds returning to their roosts atop wires and thorn trees, and I daresay, to digest the aftermath of a gluttonous day.

The winter crop is harvested before the New Year begins. Once the gigantic harvester vehicle has left the fields, whole hectares of land is strewn with grain and it is a feast for all the seed eaters including Weavers, Doves, Munias, Mynahs, Crows and whatever other bird may take fancy. And near the edges of the field, mice surface furtively from their burrows, and make short sprints to gather rice in their cheeks and then stash them away in their lairs.

The winter holidays are over at Pathashaala by the first week of January and after the children arrive I become too befuddled in the proceedings of school. So my walks to enquire on the activities of the weaver population are reduced only to weekends. But it is sometime during February that the male members of the colony start sporting their breeding colours. A bright golden helmet and a bib of the adult male now gives it a 'Holier than thou' look in its troop, but the younger and immature males are marked only with specks of yellow feathers here and there, giving them a dirty and disheveled appearance.

Nesting activities commence shortly. Palmyras and Coconut trees are the most sought after for nesting as they are tall and their fronds can be shredded to fine and neat strips which are stitched together to make their characteristic nests. The colony's strength lies in its numbers and hence the birds always stick together and a single tree may host dozens of nests. Grown Babul trees and at times Prosopises are also used but the birds always head to the palms nearby for their nesting material.

Building a nest is a highly politicized activity among the Bayas. The older males are quick to occupy the shadier and safer spots on the tree leaving the juniors the precarious and windy places. Nesting material is always taken from nearby trees and never from the one being nested on. Such a tree with time starts looking so worn and bedraggled that seeing one from a mile away, you can say for certain that the Bayas have been visiting it.

First time nesters have poor beak-eye co-ordination and may battle for several minutes with a coconut leaf before they can tear away a single strip. So quite often a youngster attempts to take the easy route out. When a neighbour's nest is unattended, it quickly hops over and pulls out a string from it to use in its own. And in turns it will nick nest strips from every nest nearby and even make considerable progress with its own nest this way. But sooner or later it is caught in the act by an infuriated owner who will charge at it screaming avian expletives and gives the unscrupulous pilferer a chase of its life. After a few of such events I think the lessons are learnt and the novices learn to tear threads by themselves for their own good. But on the other hand I have definitely noticed some more virtuous sub-adults dedicatedly observe the more experienced birds at work, seeming to have a genuine interest in the art.

Apart from this intra-specific robbery, occasionally one will notice Tailor birds and Magpie robins sneak into the nest colony when the weavers are off on a collective siesta or food break, and take away a few threads.

The females for all these weeks have been spending an utopian life, exploring new feeding grounds, sightseeing in the lake beds or just chilling out by the fields while the males have been toiling away.

Male Bayas build their nests till it resembles an upturned trophy with a chinstrap down the middle. It is now time for them to invite a female to inspect the structure they have spent stitching together for so long. Her satisfaction with his workmanship will determine whether they will mate and raise a family. The whole ordeal which ensues is a very noisy affair. Either a male will have to seek out and call a prospective mate to his nest or females may come to the nest exhibit by themselves, when their erstwhile frugal life gets too boring, to see all the options available to them. The arrival of the opposite sex sparks enormous excitement amidst the nest builders, who clutch at their respective nests and flutter their wings desperately, screeching to be the female's first choice. Even those males who have only managed to weave a few knots together on a leaf pointlessly shout out to the female to catch its attention. Probably it is just the high they feel on seeing a girl.

The shabby and loose mass of strings stitched by the sub-adults is not even given a second glance. But on settling on a more prospective nest, the female first grips the outside and tugs it around, assessing it for strength and tightness. Then there follows an inspection of the interior design after which it perches on the chinstrap and gauges the view outside from it's would be home. As all this scrutiny is taking place, the architect of the nest hangs-on outside fluttering nervously and uttering feeble chirps of persuasion to the lady.

However, few inspections take place as smoothly as described. Upon the lady's decision to give her attention to a particular male's nest, hell breaks loose in the colony. All of the other males vehemently yell out their jealous protests. At this point, the more timid females would fly away from the spot terrified by the pandemonium. Those who stay despite it and continue their examination with a growing interest, incite greater opposition. In turns, the other males may mock charge at the female to dissuade it more strongly or may try to assault the male, the nest's owner. Enraged by this the owner may launch his own attack in retaliation on one of his rivals. Furiously pecking and clawing each other, both males come revolving to the ground. Some fights persist on the floor for a while as well, leaving behind a fluff of white and yellow down feathers. In the mean time the female up on the tree may have lost interest and flown away or would have changed loyalties to another handsome nest nearby, which ofcourse instigates a fresh bout of demonstrations on the tree.

In April, the summer vacations begin as the school term comes to an end and I can resume my wanderings with greater freedom as often I am the only one residing on campus.

More often than not, the female Bayas are quite unsatisfied with the homes they've been presented with. So they fly away in outright disgust, leaving the male begging and beseeching behind her heels. Now the unfortunate creature has to start laboring again on a brand new nest, after abandoning the rejected piece. Several such rejected works hang from a nesting site, but I suspect that some unskilled and younger builders at times refurbish these and re-present them to a new lady.

On the occasions that a male is successful in impressing his mate with his workmanship, the female aids him to complete the nest. One hole of his upturned goblet is cupped to make an egg chamber and the other hole is weaved with a tunnel entrance. Happy copulation ensues, but as soon as the female begins to incubate her eggs, he begins to extend his structure to build another storey below. And if he is able to attract another girl's fancy, he will have another family right below his previous one. Once that's finished, he will start work on yet another nest. Occasionally I come across three storied nests, housing three females and their respective egg clutches. I wonder how the male deals with all his family disputes.

The nesting spree continues unfazed even through the summer, till the month of June. Exactly how many families it is that a competent male raises in a single season is a question I earnestly ponder on and am yet to address. Quite a few, no doubt. The mellow chirps of the Baya chicks now fill in between the hubbub of the adults, some of whom are still striving to accomplish one more round of procreation. The summer rice crop by June is in full seed, and it is what primarily sustains the new generation of birds. It is also at this time that the academic year begins following an onslaught of day long staff meetings. And as I get neck deep again in the hustle and bustle of teaching, the Baya flocks begin to disperse. It would be almost another six months before they flock up again and visit us, share the landscape with us and also our rice. And I am left with a feeling of gratitude for these birds for being there all through a lonely summer vacation.

A BOA OF OUR LAND

AMONGST SNAKES THE COMMON SAND BOA stands in its own rank. It has not in it the charisma of a Cobra, or the agility of a Bronzeback, the guise of a Vine snake, the stealth of a Krait or the alertness of a Rat Snake. It often comes across as a sluggish mass of flesh prowling in the night with a high level of indifference with regard to what is around it, so much so that you may squat right by it and watch it drag itself along.

The snake has on its back a dark distorted design, waxing and waning along its length which is painted on an overall sand brown complexion. Its keeled scales are as rough and protruding as it can get in snakes, making it difficult or even irritable to hold a squirming specimen. These scales also give it tremendous traction, especially the larger and pointy scales on its latter half and pulling out a snake from a bandicoot hole which is pressing itself against its walls can be an impossible task unless one digs out some of the mud around it.

The Boa then has a tail which ends in a thick blunt stub, rather than taper to a point like in most snakes and it must also be functioning as a good shovel to dig into loose sand. In dim lighting you would seriously meditate on which end of the snake that its head is held and on which end the tail, unless the snake is on the move, otherwise both ends will seem equally bulky. Not surprisingly the local folklore goes on that on every full moon (some have told me that it is during new moon, but whichever it is) the snake exchanges the position of its head and its tail. The snake does though use its tail to draw attention away from its skull when it is cornered. Go ahead and nudge the sand boa gently with a twig and you would find that it immediately jerks into a roll, its head tucked away under a coil of its body. And then, with some melodrama, it would grope about the ground with the thick end of its tail as if in search of something, like it had a mind of its own. It is actually attempting to trick you, making it seem like it is infact its other end. Now, if you were to prod the tail with a finger then out springs a head, open mouthed, from somewhere beneath the coils of its body to sink its teeth into your skin. Not to worry if you get that far. The sand boa's bite is not venomous but it isn't particularly painless either.

The Common Sand Boa can get as thick as a Casuarina's trunk and as one would anticipate it kills its prey by constriction. Don't let the name 'Boa' conjure an arboreal attribute to it. The snake strictly prefers the terra firma, largely feeding on rodents and small birds. It is a burrower, making its home in sandy terrain but is also quite often found in rubble and rock piles. And Like a true desert dweller, the Common Sand Boa also hunts by submerging its whole length in sand, but for its innocuous eyes, and lies await covertly for its quarry to venture close. Although soft sand is spoken of as its favorite grounds, I have found smaller sand boas time and again taking refuge in crab holes and stacks of clay tiles and I have found one gestating female living for several weeks deep under some planks of wet rotting wood, refusing to move and which kept returning to the same spot even after being relocated nearby.

The Common Sand Boa is an apt 'Jekyll and Hyde' snake. During the day were you to prod or pull at a sand boa in its burrow, it will give you a blank look and pretend like a log, sometimes not even attempting to move away from the disturbance. At the most it may frantically cover its head under its body or get a grip onto something near it to prevent itself from being ousted from its place. It is a dull and docile creature by the day. But come night and the snake is not at all easy going towards any leg-pulling or pranks played on it. Its eyes acquire a more vigilant look and it is quick to lose its temper and turn snappy, and will bite its aggressor with the least provocation.

The Common Sand Boa's close cousin, the Red Sand Boa, you will find a far more understanding and easy going character, only it is less frequently seen. It seldom likes to bite and moves about so placidly like no other creature in the land meant it any harm. If it was a trifle more aggressive then probably it would do a better job of dissuading its smugglers. In many villages around one frequently overhears much talk amongst the unemployed youth about making quick profits if ever they get their hands on this snake. And each time one spots the Red sand boa, there is a pang of anxiety for the creature, hoping it moves away to safety before any locals can spot it.

On a first glimpse don't mistake a Common sand boa for the formidable Russell's viper, which it poorly mimics if at all it does. Let me remind you of the perfect symmetry of the Viper's dorsal pattern, which obliquely warps and contorts on the boa's back, akin to a puerile imitation of a masterpiece. Also the chilling glare the viper gives you when it is confronted is nothing like the entirely confounded expression of the Boa. And do you think that the Viper with its fiery temperament will let you so close such that you could peer at it and take notes of its features!?

There is a certain encounter I had with the Common Sand Boa which also involved a debate over its identity and it is one I may not forget in a while. At Pathashaala, one night I was summoned from my dinner table to the office building to identify a snake which had found its way there. There was a power cut at that time and a couple of teachers, a prospective student (who was a girl of ten), her parents and their driver were standing around a moderately sized Sand boa just at the office's entrance. The school had given them an appointment early in the afternoon but they had only just arrived. When asked, I identified it as a Common sand boa, but the driver strongly voiced his disagreement to this saying that it was clearly a *KathiriViriyan* (Russell's Viper in Tamil) and cautioned the parents to clutch on safely to their daughter. I thought I will explain to him in vivid detail. So I picked up the snake and intended to hold its head so as to make it still. As the light was dim, with snake in hand, I requested the little girl who was carrying an Ipad in her hands to shine some light and aid me. I expected her to have shined the light on the snake so that seeing it, let alone catching it, becomes easier. She however showed the bright screen of the device on my face! Blinded, I put my thumb into the snake's jaws like a pacifier into a baby's mouth. The debate over the snake didn't continue after this, but after seeing me suffer no excruciating pain or a bulging finger or tissue necrosis, I suppose the man changed his mind regarding the identity of the snake. And the next day I found two fine transparent teeth from the snake's extensive dentition still jutting out from my thumb.

KNOW YOUR LARKS

Drifting clouds...
the song of a Skylark
over the paddyfields

WHEN YOU TAKE A WALK IN ANY SOUTH INDIAN country side you would have unfailingly noticed among other birds, a brown sparrow sized one, streaked with black all over its chest and mantle, as if it were done with a very fine tipped paintbrush. It would either be sitting on a wire, on a mud road or on a low leafless branch. There are few other places where it may choose to sit. A rather non-descript and shy little bird which will crouch into its seat, bury it's neck into its shoulders and freeze if you passed by, hoping that it will go unnoticed but then would flit away diffidently if you turned around and caught sight of it. You would probably appreciate yourself for having had the eye to have even noticed such a bird, only and only till it leaps into the air, several meters high, and on reaching the apex, parachutes down with its short wings out-stretched whilst uttering a series of shrill pitch perfect whistles. It lands now on a different bush or a different part of a fence, catches its breath and just when you would think that the bird is done with its display, it will leap forth into the air again and sing another succession of sweet whistles. Hear though that it whistles exactly thirteen or fourteen times during it descent. If its jump happened to fall short a bit then it would continue calling even after it has perched but the number of its calls remain constant. If you did bump into such a bird on your countryside wanderings then you have met with a Jerdon's Bushlark. And this is how this lark calls out for a partner every morning.

Down south, winter doesn't imply snow or hail or several layers of dense woolen clothing. Winter here means misty mornings, much colder than usual, frequent rains and rainbows, enormous cumulonimbuses and pleasantly warm afternoons. And when I sit back and haul in memories of this season, among the first images which come to mind are of the Bush larks in the hazy distance rising up and drifting down over the Prosopis bushes, their calls echoing diffusely through the land like the sounds from Buddhist singing bowls. But they do these displays right from the advent of winter by the year's end, every morning for the next three or four months. Why do they consistently pursue this activity? Does a female watch the males for days and days before making its choice? Does it take many years of practice for a male to flawlessly execute this airborne feat? I am of this impression. For one sees some birds jump reluctantly into the air and then come down on jittery wings rotating back and forth to maintain their balance and some others, probably the more experienced males, hover to high heights and then drift down smoothly on effortless wings, quite perfectly timing their whistles and their landing.

Again if you are a commoner of the country side you would have seen if not known, and certainly heard if not seen two other equally jubilant and widespread species of the lark tribe.

The Oriental Skylark by appearance is indistinguishable from a Jerdon's to a layman's eye but the male wears a Mohawk like crest which it can flatten and erect at will. But what really tells larks apart from a mile away are their distinct courting flights. The Skylark ascends high into the heavens till it is a tiny blotch or at times not visible at all, and then showers its song down from there while it hovers on its little pinions. It renders a lengthy improvisation which is modulated by the wind currents giving it varying dynamics, muffling its voice now and then making it loud and clear moments later, like it was playing around with the volume knob. The winds make its song more enchanting as it plays on our ears but its currents are what the bird fights, as they keep carrying it away downwind while the bird struggles to stay put where it chose to be. On a gloomy day a Skylark's spirited song is quite enough to lift one's spirits and so also did Shelley express in his "To a Skylark"-

"Better than all measures
Of delightful sound,
Better than all treasures
That in books are found,
Thy skill to poet were, thou scorner of the ground!"

"Teach me half the gladness
That thy brain must know,
Such harmonious madness
From my lips would flow
The world should listen then, as I am listening now."

Now for how long do the bird's renditions last in the sky? As I sat in the grass outside the field, endlessly waiting for my turn of batting to come during the weekend morning cricket matches at Pathashaala, I better occupied my time by timing the skylarks which would be performing right over the play grounds. They would preen themselves before and come to rest between performances right on the pavilion we were sitting on. They would sing in the skies for an average of seven to ten minutes, occasionally touching fifteen. But again some would do only a couple of minutes like it were just a rehearsal. The winds too play a role on the length of a Skylark's song. In the mornings when the weather is quite placid these birds stay in the air for considerably longer as compared to the afternoons when the currents are erratic and hostile. Listen carefully to a Skylark's song and you will find that it is clearly an amalgamate of many birds found in the same landscape, whose calls it listens and learns and duplicates in its own voice. Listen and now you hear a Francolin, then a Thick-knee, then a Lapwing merged after it seamlessly, then a Prinia or even a Jerdon's Bushlark. When the birds reach the limit of their endurance, they would point to the ground and begin a nose dive. They would fall freely on limp wings for over a hundred feet and you will bite your lip the first time you watch one, thinking for sure that it is going to smash on the ground at its terminal velocity. But just a few feet from the floor, the skylark would whisk up and flutter, dip and rise and land somewhere in the grass. The birds take a brief respite, eat some grain, visit a rain puddle, straighten out and put their feathers right and set off skyward again.

The other lark you must acquaint yourself with is the Ashy Crowned Sparrow-Lark. The male is deep smoke colored with a bandit like black patch on its eyes while the female is an innocuous grey. Its bill is thicker like a sparrow's and its shoulders wider and strongly built. And it too has a graceful courting display to offer the female and us too, if we sit and watch, putting aside our wearisome errands. It flies up into the air and swoops in long inverted parabolas while voicing a soft mellifluous whistle, which rises as the bird falls and falls as the bird rises. Sometimes several males display within close proximity and there is a mesmerizing succession of eternally waxing and waning whistles, lulling, calming and something one can listen to all through the afternoon till sundown.

A FROG WHICH RUNS ON WATER

THE COMMON BASILISK FOUND IN THE rainforests of Central and South America is also called by the name Jesus Christ Lizard. When the lizard sees a threat it is known to run to the closest water body and continue running on the water's surface for a short distance using its large buoyant feet. That being said, do we all know that there is such a creature, which can perform the same miracle, in each of our ponds, ditches and wells? It's a frog however and has modestly been named the Skittering frog but I am certain that if it had been subjected to enough biblical influence, it would have been named the Jesus Christ frog much before, given its omnipresence.

I distinctly remember the first time I came upon the skittering frog. It was a long time back, when I was in grade seven and when I had gone on a school trip to Thiruvannamalai. As part of the trip we went to a place where afforestation activities were being done. During a walk there alone I happened to loiter near a murky cattle pond and peer into it. A frog which had been sitting at the pond's edge, on seeing me, turned and fled by taking quick steps on the water with its hind legs while holding its forelegs near its chest and suddenly disappeared beneath the surface. I was nothing less than wonderstruck for I had stumbled upon a creature which could run on water! I threw little pebbles where the frog had vanished to see if it may surface again. Then I immediately ran along and dragged back with me a friend to show him what I had found. To my vexation I couldn't find that frog along the entire edge of the pond and my comrade began to wonder whether my description was all cock and bull. What I had seen still felt unreal to me and I now slightly began to suspect my own memory. As I continued looking around he turned finicky for it was getting close lunchtime. However on my adamant insistence he joined me on a walk around the pond and alas we found numerous more Skittering frogs on the other side of the pond, each of which clearly sprinted over the water's surface one after the other as we walked along, exemplifying for my dear friend that the creature I spoke of indeed existed.

Skittering frogs are happy residing in any standing body of water however murky and dirty they maybe. Stagnant pools in a stream bed, wells, lakes and ponds. You can see them floating serenely in ditches and open sewers as well. And they are quick to occupy large enough puddles too, left behind by the rains. Overnight they abruptly appear like the rest of the frogs after the first heavy downpour of the monsoon disrupts their summer slumber. These frogs are patched with dirty green blotches on an overall soil brown complexion, as if they are wearing an army uniform tailored to their dimensions. Unlike a Bull frog or a Paddyfield frog, the Skitterers don't venture too far away from the water in search of their food. At the most they may come to the water's edge to bask in the slush, but even then the toes of their hind legs may still be touching the water, ever ready to turn and scoot backwards, if danger came their way. As the sun begins to set and the waters begin to get colder, especially in the winter months, I have seen these frogs convene on a lotus or a lily pad sitting around and over one another, and I think they spend the nights that way. But otherwise for most of the day, a Skittering frog floats in the water and like a crocodile, only its eyes and snout breaking the surface, motionless, only letting itself be bobbed up and down by gentle ripples, till an unsuspecting water skater glides temptingly close to it.

Lotus pond...
a frog's
long silence

The call of a Skittering frog is distinctly recognizable amidst the notes, chords, yells and inflections of a nocturnal Anuran cacophony. It sounds just like the loud consequence of flatulence and I can't think of a more apt description. By the cement parapet above the little stream which weaves through Pathashaala, I take the pleasure of sitting on for a while before dinner. When the stream begins to run dry after many months of gushing flow, its craters hold small pools which are now dense with whatever amphibious life remains. Dozens of Skitterers float here with a transfixed gaze towards the sky. And as daylight fades away, one call is heard, then another and another and then all together, some in succession, some in synchrony, and all of them participate in the night long dialogue. At times I too try to join in. I vibrate my lips loudly, trying to mimic them. A short silence befalls. I repeat my impressions and one or two in sometime will voice their calls, either in response or on their own, and the rest join in.

The largest pool, just below the cement parapet was also home then to two Checkered keelback snakes, one large adult and a smaller juvenile. These snakes lived somewhere inside the culvert over which a mud path bridged both banks of the stream for us to cross over. After the rains had receded, these snakes would show their heads only after dusk. They would lie on the large cement culverts which protruded underneath the path for a while, imbibing the last light from the western horizon before they went out on their prowl. Occasionally the snakes would have a go at the floating frogs but I have never seen them catch one. They would enter the water slyly as if they never noticed the frogs, let alone having any thoughts of eating them. Then one snake would fix its unblinking focus on a single one, and propel itself forward in the water towards it. The frog would have had its eyes on it all the while and would begin its sprint on the water. All the other frogs would flee in every other direction, making a loud noise as if someone threw a bucket of sand in the pool. The snake would undulate its body more rapidly forward now, trying to force the frog to flee towards land where it would be easy meat. When the snake has it within reach, just at the right moment, the frog would abruptly plop itself vertically below into the water, while the snake's momentum casts it well beyond where its prey all of a sudden disappeared. Meanwhile the frog dives to the bottom of the pool and swipes a blanket of mud over it, making the water around murky. It remains hidden there till the cloud of mud settles down by itself again. The snake gives up on this one and has a few more tries with a couple of other frogs. The process repeats and the snake only ends up throwing itself about here and there in the water. It then gives up all together and crawls on to the land to look for easier prey. When stillness returns to the pool and the snakes are out of sight, the Skittering frogs rise up to the surface and resume floating and croaking again.

Bel plants and Lime Caterpillars – A Lime butterfly lays its eggs near a social spiders' web.

Lime plants and Bel caterpillars – An older Lime caterpillar eats its earlier garb

The Song of a Whistling Thrush – A Whistling Thrush seated on its podium

A Pink bird with a Persona – A short melee between the adult birds

Some attributes of a Rat snake – Raising its body for a better view

Another Sketch of a Roller – A Roller dries its wings after a drizzle

The Thrush and the Pitta – A Pitta standing cross legged deep in the vegetation

The Thrush and the Pitta – An Orange Headed Thrush with a look of scrutiny

Egglay Delay – A female Tawny Coster laying its eggs

As Calm as a Toad – A puny male attempts to subdue a much larger female

Acquainting with the Bronzeback – A Bronzeback making its way through thorns and brambles

The Life in a Paddyfield – A flock of Openbills foraging in a paddyfield

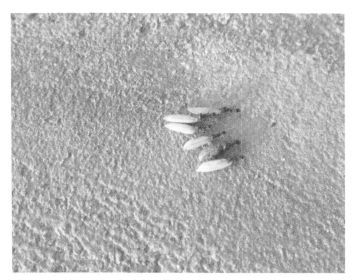

The Life in a Paddyfield – Ants return to their nest with fresh grain after the harvest

A Brief Calendar of Baya Weavers – Males clutch their nests and screech out to a female

A Boa of our Land – The countenance of a Common Sand Boa

Know your Larks – A Jerdon's Bushlark perched atop a termite hill

Know your Larks – The male Ashy-Crowned Sparrow Lark

A Frog which runs on water – A Skitterer spending time on a lotus pad

BULLY ANTS AND GRAM BLUES

THERE IS A VERDANT PATCH OF WILD GRAM (Vigna trilobata) just by the stone paved pathway between the classrooms and the common toilet, at Pathashaala. With the first monsoon showers the little plants break the soil's surface, grow and blossom. They are there to stay for the next six or seven months before drying up into the soil again. Their leaves are prostrate but the small yellow flowers, which are like little folded up ribbons and their long pods are held high above the ground by a thin green stem. Some books refer to this plant also as the Three-Lobe-Leaved Cowpea, which is quite a mouthful yet very descriptive of it nevertheless.

Formidable hordes of Black bully ants (Camponotus compressus) nest just underground, their tunnels and cloisters are scaffolded by the roots of Wild gram. The bites of these ants have more muscle than acid and their mandible sizes equal that of their legs. If you ever saw one biting you or someone else, you would certainly have noticed that the ant bites with such brute force that often its abdomen and hind legs lift off the floor when it does. I was enlightened later that these ants have a great fondness for urea and hence I understood why invariably their nests are close to toilets.

Gram blue butterflies play hide and seek among these plants too. These are neat gray butterflies, with colorless dots and curves on the underwings at the tip of which are two orange crowned black spots which look like a little pair of gleaming eyes when the insect sits upside down. The male woos behind the female as she weaves through the plants avoiding him, and explores his prospects with her. The lady I suppose looks for sustained determination and perseverance in her partner in this slow courting chase before agreeing to mate with him. These romance rituals happen in this specific place for a reason. The Gram blues lay their eggs on the tender flower buds of the Wild Gram. And after August, at any given time during the day you will find dozens of females fluttering about, looking for buds and laying eggs. The emergence of the caterpillar from its egg marks the beginning of a fierce bond, an enduring symbiosis between the ant and the caterpillar.

During the lunch breaks and free periods, I come and sit on the stone pathway to watch the activities of the ants and the caterpillars. This would also be the time when the common toilet would receive maximum attendance. My observations would be continually disrupted by people who find me sprawled orthogonally in their way. I would be perpetually asked to kindly move aside and often urgently so.

The soldiers of the Bully ants which are patrolling the patch immediately sense the presence of a new caterpillar once it has hatched and discover its whereabouts. A new born caterpillar is maroonish like the flower buds of the Wild Gram, which it hides in and devours from the inside and the creature is about the size of a rice kernel. With some growth, the caterpillar turns green with a black head like a mustard seed. Now the full time, self assigned job of the ants is to be the body guards of the caterpillars, staying close to it, following behind it wherever it roams on the plant and to militantly defend it from its predators. Sometimes you may find upto three ants guarding a single caterpillar, following it closely from behind, beneath and by the side. They also constantly tap their antennae on the caterpillar's body and sometimes this seems to guide the movements of the caterpillar. This I think is the medium of communication between these two organisms, the language of antennae tapping. And possibly the caterpillar also replies to the ants by way of unique contractions and convulsions of its torso. Along with the buds, the caterpillars go for the tender seed pods of the plant too. They nibble a small entry into the pod at its end attached to the stalk and enter it. Once inside, the larvae sedulously munch away every single seed all along the length of the seed pod. And as it is doing so, the ant stands guard outside covering the hole, till the caterpillar crawls out of the seed pod again.

The ants work in shifts to guard the caterpillar, like the professional security personnel of our own kind. Another will climb up the plant to relieve the one which has been on duty for all this while. And I have confirmed that they render their security during the night as well during my nocturnal visits to the toilet after a night show movie. An ant as it is, has enough work to do for its colony in a day, right from scouting for food, bringing it to the nest, maintaining the nest and guarding it and God knows what all else. I find it rather extraordinary, even inspiring infact, that over and above all this they fit in the time to guard the caterpillars as well. From an ant one can learn the importance and inward significance of working for a larger purpose, for a greater good. Only a larger purpose, whatever it may be, gives one the strength and spirit to strive untiringly all day, every day, for a goal larger than oneself. In return for the ant's services, the larvae regularly provide them with honey dew, a sugar rich liquid which they secrete from the New Comer's gland found on their backs. The ants put their forelegs on the caterpillar and gladly gulp it down their mandibles.

As far as I have seen, no birds seek out these caterpillars. They are concealed within petals or pods most of the time and to many birds they are barely a mouthful and aren't worth taking the trouble to find. Even Prinias and Zitting Cisticolas for whom this patch of Wild Gram mixed with tall grass and knotted creepers, is a standard feeding ground all day, I have seen only go away with larger prey like mantises, grasshoppers and spiders. I believe that more than any other creature, the principal hunters of these caterpillars are the parasitic wasps. They seek them out and inject them with their eggs using their hooked needle-like ovipositors. The wasp larvae then devour the caterpillar from within and emerge as adult wasps from its decaying body. One afternoon I saw an Ichneumon wasp alight on a plant on which a caterpillar was resting under the shade of a flower. Whether it landed there by coincidence or knowing a caterpillar was there I couldn't say. Two ants were there by the caterpillar's side. As soon as the plant shook with the wasp's arrival, the more massive ant charged at it with wide open mandibles, with every intention to finish it off. Noticing its assailant approaching, the wasp flew away for dear life. It was apparent that both clearly recognized one another and their intentions. But it is not that the ants attack anything living or dead which happens to land on the plant. To the adult Gram Blue butterflies which came to lay eggs on the plant or which happened to be basking on them, the ants were completely indifferent to. Nor did they mind the chrysomelid beetles which grazed on the leaves underneath, which mean no harm to the caterpillars.

When I grow weary of passive, unobtrusive observation, I decide to investigate into the ant's protective behavior a trifle further and I have ended up learning much about to what extents it will go to defend the caterpillar it has assigned itself to. If I prodded the caterpillar with my finger when the ants were slightly away from it, they would come charging ferociously at it as they did to the parasitic wasp. They were quite convinced that my intentions were devious ones. After being nailed a few times, I decided I will use a thin twig to continue with my investigations. Now when I prodded the caterpillar with the twig the ant would come charging again, grab the twig and toss it aside or go down the plant and drop it down. Or in some instances it would close its jaws with such fury that the frail stick would snap into two. These twigs

I used are only the dried stems of the Wild Gram or piece of rigid Cyperus grass. Now when I lifted off the caterpillar from the plant using my twig but yet held it within reach of the ant, on several occasions it would reach out for it standing on its hinds, carry it gently between its jaws and place it back on the plant and then begin its attacks on the twig. The caterpillar seemed to be aware of the ant's actions and fatigue levels and after such a strenuous bout of activity inflicted by me on the ant it would secrete honey dew to revitalize its companion.

We live in an age where competition, domination and one-upmanship are portrayed as the crucial elements for survival. Where power and influence both subtle and glaring, are thought primarily necessary for one's deepest fulfillment and gratification. But the ant and the caterpillar, like the Honey guide and the Badger or the Hermit crab and the Sea anemone, are beacons for a different kind of community. A community where relating and relationship, synergy and symbiosis and being there for one another, are regarded above everything else.

THE WOLVES AMONG SNAKES

THIS IS THE DAY BEFORE THE FIRST DAY OF school. The children were expected to start arriving from early next morning at the campus. Two holiday months of neglect was being cleaned and washed over this last week and today it was the library's turn. Every now and then one would hear a shriek or a succession of vituperations from a teacher, because a Scorpion was found close at hand or a House Centipede had scampered over one's arm while probing into dusty book piles in the slotted angles. Two men brought in a ladder all of a sudden, as if they had lost their way and wandered in, but it was to bring down carton boxes from the loft for packing away books which were merely occupying shelf space.

One of the women staff went up the rain drenched ladder, stepping slowly on each rung, out of both caution and reluctance for having been put on the job. On finally reaching the top, she had one look into the loft and hurried down as fast as her tight Sari would allow her. She apparently had a glimpse of a snake up there which she repeatedly cried of on her way down, making all the teachers and staff-body gather below. Now the job was put on my shoulders. This was a loft which was about fifteen feet from the ground and was as big as a room by itself. No illumination found its way in there except for the thinly mottled sunlight at one corner which came through the ventilation vaults. From the wet ladder I climbed onto what could have been surely among the dustiest surfaces I had set foot on. In the light of my camera's red flash pointer I saw a Common Wolf snake, coiled tightly as if it had knotted onto itself several times, as it rested near a crowbar on the loft. The crowbar too was a surprise since it was long thought to be lost. Fragments of the snake's shed skin stretched across the walls and the dusty articles above. This periodically forgotten space has evidently been its residence for quite some time now. Would it return here and hide after each night's hunt, making its way up the wall and through the ventilation holes? Or did it confine itself here, feeding on Geckos and their eggs and whatever other creatures which lived in this large dark space? Was this snake a recluse having sought hermitage in this loft? It was clearly getting enough to eat as this was among the largest and girthiest Wolf snakes I had seen. Its thickness, in the dim light, could have made it easily be mistaken for a modestly sized Checkered Keelback if not for its precarious perch.

Holding a gunny sack nearby, I nudged the sleeping snake towards it. Without any fuss, the snake crept straight into a snug corner of the sack. I then pretended to walk towards the campus gate to release the snake outside but took a turnabout, when all the eyes had gone back to their work, and let the snake free by a rubble heap just behind the library, so that it could climb back again to its former dwelling once the bustle of activity up there ended. Several months later I had to go up the loft again to bring down a large steel box. I hoped to see the Wolf snake again but I couldn't sight it from my superficial search. Its withered skins were still there, coming away in flakes. Probably it had gone away and found shelter elsewhere. Or probably it was still living in the dusty depths of the loft, in a corner which would seldom be searched.

By nature the Wolf snake is rebellious. And it is reputed to forthcomingly protest while being relocated. It adores entering buildings or human quarters and takes up lodgings in some neglected corner or junk pile. Some typical places of their preference are rolled up mats, stick brooms and under dust gathering wooden articles and furniture. When unexpectedly discovered in its hideout, the snake gets downright furious. It jumps like a cornered Rottweiler, making resolute attacks to clamp its jaws shut on its aggressor, no matter how outsized it may be. I was once giving my room a thorough sweeping after a long field trip and wasn't aware that in the meantime, a Common Wolf snake had made its abode under my bureau. When it got prodded by the broom's end, the snake neither attempted to flee nor did it freeze in its place to wait for danger to pass, as any other more timid snake would have done. While walking to the other end of the room I found my new roommate hanging by its teeth from the broom's end. It chewed with vengeance on the broom's bristles like it was its sole enemy. Well it made it easy for me to carry it out.

The Common Wolf snake's close cousin is an entirely different personality altogether. The Barred wolf snake occurs in all the places where the Common Wolf snake may occur but is always less frequently seen. It also may not enter our quarters as much. However, following the floods of December 2015, I was involved in a snake rescue spree around the school and in houses in the villages around during when numerous snakes had taken refuge in huts, school buildings and the like. And I found Barred wolf snakes as commonly as Common wolf snakes, that I am now of the impression that they are just more shy and furtive in their whereabouts, which makes them more difficult to sight.

A Barred wolf snake is a gentle creature and never likes to bite. But it tries making up for it tender-heartedness through its mimicry and dramatics. A cornered individual will jerk into strike position and execute a few half hearted mock jumps. Disturbed further and it will roll into a tight concentric coil with its head hidden somewhere beneath. But infact it is secretly watching you, keeping a careful eye on your movements, for if you walk around it, it will quickly shift its head under another coil of its body to keep you within its view and its vibrating tail tip will follow your location like a compass needle. When it feels that its attacker is not paying attention, its head peeks out to have a quick glance around and then the snake will frantically slither away for dear life, showing its true colors.

And when one speaks of colours, it needs mention that a Barred Wolf snake can look deceptively similar to a little Common Krait. This venomous snake is by no means tolerated by any of the locals. The Krait is notorious for biting sleeping victims. One of the senior farming staff here at school claims that he lost three of his uncles to this snake this way and walks every night with a long stick, perpetually seeking revenge. And two in three of his kills would be Barred Wolf snakes. Yes I have tried pointing out some differences between the two. But I realize that the poor man's mental baggage is just too much, from all the bitter memories and the family disputes and property fights which ensued as ramifications after the snake bite, that I mostly leave him to his ways. But a Common Krait has large hexagonal scales running all along its back which the Wolf snake lacks, albeit this is a trifle of detail which won't be the first thing which usually occurs to someone when he or she stumbles upon a snake. Also look for bands starting right after the head in a Wolf snake and Rosette markings all along its flanks which you won't see on the Krait. The other day a colleague rung on my phone and woke me up, during his night walk around the campus, saying that he is standing in front of a snake which was black with white bands. I shared the pointers of difference between the Krait and the Wolf snake. But he said he wasn't able to clearly see any of these and insisted that I come to the spot and help him identify it. When I went there I discovered my genuinely short sighted colleague standing with caution some thirty feet away from an elastic rope cord, the one with hooks on either end, flung by the walkway.

OF GULLS AND TERNS

FOR A RELAXED WEEKEND BIRDING TRIP, I GO TO the backwaters of Mutthukadu some twenty five kilometers from Chennai city. En route there is the Kelambakkam backwater as well on either side of the highway by which one can pull over or slow down one's vehicle to witness the profusion of birdlife. Here the ocean makes a broad intrusion into land which runs several kilometers inside. Mutthukadu too is a part of this stretch. On the way to Mahabalipuram, on the East coast road, stop before the trembling bridge which connects the two. Adjacent to the bridge is a boathouse on whose piers I sit and watch over the backwater. Or sometimes I would take a circuitous route along the beach and sit at the mouth where the ocean enters the land, where the place is tranquilly devoid of noisy motor boats and its hysterical passengers. Between November and March and even a bit into April, one can see here all the migrant shorebirds from their respective countries, passing the winter on our warmer coasts.

For the larger part of the backwaters, the water is atmost shin deep and the bird density is greatest here, despite being flanked by tall apartments, construction sites and a noisy road. Sand flats and sizeable dunes border the backwaters where it meets the Bay of Bengal. Fishermen cast their nets as they traverse through the sinking mud under the shallow seawater and a large canal emptying into the backwaters, by the boat house, brings with it sewage from the township around. Watching the fisherman, I once took off my shoes and tried entering the water from the boathouse with my pendulously cumbersome camera hanging on my neck. Here the silt was so fine and slippery that I skid and danced in the water with my very second step and then earned a strong warning from the boathouse staff.

In these waters one will find birds of both wetlands and the shore. If you are there close to sunrise you may still see flocks of gulls, some floating on water, bobbing up and down, and some sitting on the sand banks mostly on one leg, on the shallow side of the coast where the waves don't beat the beach. With them you will find scattered here and there, Caspian terns, with their bright red beaks being the most striking features of the entire shore line. They are soon on the wing, once the water currents are warm enough. I was enlightened by a fisherman there that a backwater being more stagnant than the sea is always colder, so most of the fish move out during the night and come back in after sunrise. Where the water is deeper Pelicans sail around with their glowing pouches, eyeing the water close to the surface and then abruptly engulfing a copious quantity of it, which is filtered between ridges in its beak to swallow only the fish without all the ten liters of saltwater it filled its mouth with. There are cormorants too sticking only their necks above the surface which will brusquely sink underneath and then reappear ten feet away in any direction. Where it is shallower you will find Grey herons, Storks, Egrets and Pond herons standing gazing down below ready to spear in their bills when a fish passes by. The little egrets are often solitary hunters. But suddenly someday you will see them hunting in a small group of three or four with an ingenious strategy. One or two will fly above a shoal of fish rallying them to shallower waters where they are easier to catch. Others lying in waiting now come over and grab a fish for themselves till the shoal disperses. Again a bird or two will take off and gather the fish to a convenient spot and the others quickly fly over and clutch their share. You will also find Plovers and Sandpipers scurrying along where the waterline touches the sand and a few pairs of Pied Kingfishers have been permanent residents in little mud tunnels found along the steep edges of the waste water canal.

Spring tide …
a wave tosses up
a flock of gulls

By afternoon most of the birds resign and laze around in the shallows and mud mounds with tucked necks, tilted heads and stretched wings and it is only the Gulls and Terns you will see active and on the wing almost throughout the day. They relentlessly quarter over the water looking for fish or fry. When a Caspian Tern spots a fish and intends to go for it, it utters a hoarse shriek, drifts upwards and then plummets vertically down with stretched out feet towards its prey.

So if you fancy taking photos of diving birds breaking the water surface, this tern gives you a clear cue before it is going to, for you to turn your attention and then focus and click. The gull hunts similarly but is a silent entity. Now watch closely as these birds catch their fish. They both have a unique method they employ to do so. They don't pick them off with their talons like an Osprey or a Fish eagle nor do they thrust down their bills like a Kingfisher, with singular accuracy. As a Tern or a Gull breaks the surface of the water at the finish of its dive, it spreads both its webbed feet around its prey, cupping it inside with the water and confining it within so that grabbing it then becomes easier. At closer quarters I have seen some fish escape by jumping out of the cup.

The sleeker body and the sharper wings of a Tern give it more airborne maneuverability than a Gull. It can stall itself instantly if it sees its quarry, turn sharply on a curve in pursuit over a fish and is less at the mercy of the winds. Their dives are quicker too and their proportion of successful catches in comparison to the blunt winged gulls is on any day, significantly higher. So the Gulls in order to even out these differences have become the bully boys around here. If a Gull is not having much luck catching its own fish then it will glide about slowly keeping one eye on a tern nearby. Once the tern returns from the water with a fish in its mouth, the gull swerves around and pursues it calling out rudely behind its heels. The Tern will try its best to swallow its meal whole before its nemesis gets to it or it may just drop it for the Gull to pick up, to avoid any loss of feathers. But more common than these scenarios are intra species hounding, wherein a Tern mobs a Tern or a Gull mobs a Gull to snatch the other's rightful catch.

Sitting by these backwaters and watching these birds, if one is to learn anything, see anything at all, it is important to practice watching, dropping all past memories, past experiences. Watch yourself when you see a bird. You see how tempted the mind feels to give the creature a name, put a noun, a label on it and then hastily shift its glance to something else. It is a psychologically arduous task to watch a bird without any memory of it, moreover, to consider what it truly means to be the bird. How would it have felt to have flown over the landscapes of several continents to reach this Bay? How would it be to catch and swallow fish day after day to keep alive? How would it be to float with the sea breeze on still pinions? A mind not caught in naming or describing, which is still and totally watching, for sometime fully becomes a Gull or a Tern and for sometime inhabits an entirely different world.

LESSON PLANS AROUND A TREE

THE NATURALIST ROBERT MICHAEL PYLE STATED IN his book, The Thunder Tree, that "One of the greatest causes of the ecological crisis is the state of personal alienation from nature." I feel he has articulated the most fundamental issue in our times, the lack of a direct relationship with the larger environment, a deeply personal one. This personal touch by a long way precedes policies, laws and conservation. Nothing substitutes the experience of nature, of wilderness, by being present in it and on one's own terms. The complete sensorial witnessing of it which also sinks in beyond.

For biology and EVS teachers, I included, it is immensely difficult to incorporate this element of creating frames for students to learn and discover from nature while we also hurry with academic portions and manage our other responsibilities. Yes most often the reins of syllabi, curricula and timetables are just too constraining and they make you feel like a pancake on a conveyor belt. But despite all of this, in the few and far between spaces for us to experiment, think and be creative, we have all strived to integrate our lessons with the larger environment.

The older children find nature, trees and birds somehow unfashionable and outdated and they will spend their time talking about their clothing, football matches or things of that sort if one takes them on nature walks. I have found it much easier to experiment with new ideas while teaching middle school.

Taking inspiration from the Buddhist saying "You are not a single drop in the ocean but the ocean in a single drop," as an enthusiastic science teacher, I wondered if all the principles of ecology and the various relationships in an ecosystem could be understood by studying a single tree or a plant and the life it hosts. My other inspiration was Eleanor Duckworth's principle of making 'Nature as the Teacher' or the direct resource person. I mention here my experiences while toying with this idea and the learnings I observed taking place.

I called it a 'Creature hunt' so as to make it sound less detestable to fifth and sixth graders. I split the mixed age class into groups of three or four students and each small group is allotted a tree for their study. On the campus of Pathashaala, Pongamia trees are in plenty, and if different groups are allotted the same species there is an opportunity for them to compare notes with eachother later on. I give each group about half an hour or more with their respective tree/plant. During this time their objective is to take an inventory of all the creatures they find on their tree; bugs, caterpillars, birds if any, on the branches, the trunk, beneath the leaves and anywhere else on the tree. It helps immensely if I visit the tree before hand to plan and then before the activity begins, to give a generic picture of what the children can expect to find if they are observant and if they scour through the leaves and branches meticulously enough. And also as a priming element and to aid them identify and feel like little taxonomists, I tell them how a butterfly, moth and a sawfly and their larvae differ from each other, how to distinguish leaf hoppers from beetles, between crab spiders and lynx spiders and other notable pointers based on my own observations. And if there is some species which is found only during that season, like a Warbler or the Black Rajah butterfly, it helps to just make a passing comment saying "let us see which group is lucky enough to spot these rarities."

The clarity and conviction with which one gives children instructions for the larger part determines their engagement with the activity and saves one's efforts in managing all the tangents and digressions which may crop up later. Treat instructions like making a public speech and rehearse it the previous night. Write it on the board. Print them on pieces of paper and distribute them. If possible get it engraved on a block of stone!

At their trees, the students fill up three columns for each critter they spot on a worksheet I give them; what they think it is, a short description of it, to help them recall it later, and a line about what it was doing. It can be surprising, the sense of adventure which is instilled in them when kids sift through branches looking for a new species. I usually go around with my camera visiting each group, to photograph any interesting findings. These can be projected on screen later and the groups can share their work with the whole class. But I also do this because each time atleast one of the groups discovers something on the tree which is new even to me. But even if I didn't go around, I would be hand dragged to the spot if any of them came across something they found intriguing. Once I was shown a predatory bug on the Pongamia with a long proboscis (which I later got identified by experts as an Eocanthecona furcellata) which impaled the larvae of other insects and sucked out their body fluids. It was a lifer for me. So was the warning display of the Sunbeam butterfly's caterpillar brought to my notice this way. The creature would shoot out two black hairy ribbons from false antennae on its posterior when the students nudged it with a pen. This task reaps the best benefits if it is done after summer when the Pongamia trees are still bearing flowers and when the insect activity is at its peak. Any plant or tree for that matter should do during this time of the year. My second most favorite plants to assign for this activity are Morning Glories in full bloom, teaming with Tortoise shell bugs and Blister beetles. I remember the way a little girl once pointed out to me how the Marsh dartlet damselflies waited outside the Morning glory flowers and caught the flies which came to visit them. And I remember the way she smiled at the flowers when she was looking at them.

Back in the classroom, after all the field work is over, I keep whatever field guides are available, for butterflies, birds, spiders and so on, and the groups are given some time to try and identify as many species as they can. If not that at least the possible family or the order based on the descriptions they have put down. The chaos which ensues in the room is a healthy one and the teacher too can join in as a resource. Then the class gathers and each group takes turns to share their learnings and findings.

The academic scope of such an activity is vast and a range of exercises can be set to reinforce the run of the mill syllabus objectives. Beyond building food chains and webs from their observations, trophic levels and biomass pyramids can be discussed in this context. The implications of causing an imbalance of a particular species in the tree ecosystem can be thought about. The adaptations of different species can be noted and questions like which species was best adapted and which was least adapted for survival on the tree can be raised and debated over. Ecological terms like predation, competition, parasitism, symbiosis, etc, can be introduced and the interactions observed on the tree can be classified based on this. Different keys for the organisms can be made based on various criteria.

Lesson plans of a similar nature can be constructed around other outdoor activities, like using quadrats and short transect walks on a given path. Quadrats especially lend to comparing different landscapes and creature compositions. Individual and silent observation instead of group activity also carries its own benefits and ensuing discussions, of a different kind. One could ask children to also observe the flow of their thoughts, the different sensations on their limbs and bodies during this time and ask if the tree played a role in any of this.

When a tree is used as a resource, the learning is carried beyond the classroom. Many kids will have a look under a branch or at a cocoon under a leaf on their way to lunch or when walking to the games field. Once in a while you will be pulled away by your students, while you are correcting papers or enjoying your day off, to show you something new they found. Or worse, they may bring the creature into the staffroom. And I constantly have had to deal with that. But the most profound value of such an activity is the possibility that later on, the child will always find the time to be in touch with a plant or a tree.

ITCHES, INFLAMMATIONS AND OTHER CATERPILLAR DEFENSES

I BROUGHT TO MY ROOM ONE EARLY WINTER'S morning, a small cutting of the Sage-Leaved Alangium tree which hosted on its leaves a full batch of Nettle Moth caterpillars (Parasa lepida). These caterpillars have green and white stripes alternating along the length of their bodies with clumps of tiny dark pricks on the head, rear and all across their flanks. They are fatter than they are long and have the merest vestiges of legs, or rather mild bumps beneath them, making each one look like a cross between a slug and a marshmallow. The leisurely pace at which the creature moves in life, owes to the fact that no predator dares to touch it. In theory I knew that these creatures, if brushed with, can give among the most awful itches one may have the misfortune of contracting.

The Alangium cuttings didn't last long in my glass jars, even when well watered, so in a few days I had to provide the caterpillars a new branch to feed from. I could have thought of a ten different ways to transfer the caterpillars to their fresh fodder without having to touch them. But how could these tiny creatures, hardly half the length of my little finger, affect my tough manly hide? Such trifling thoughts of precautions would only occur to ones with delicate skins in constant need of sun screens and fairness creams, was what my bloated mind suggested to me. After manually relocating only a few caterpillars, my fingertips began to tingle slightly. Unthinkingly I used one of them to scratch the insides of my nose. Very shortly my hands started to sting but they were by many orders of magnitude more tolerable than my nose which felt like it had just caught on fire. My nostrils had considerably widened and by the way my nasal septum throbbed, I was sure it was going to split into two along its length. On the mirror, the middle chunk of my face was as florid as a circus clown's. Lacto Calamine lotion was completely ineffective. I poured into my nose the only other thing available in my bathroom which I thought may give some relief, Dettol solution, and I choked on it. In about half an hour's time, spent twitching on my bed, face flat over a pillow, the burning subsided to normal as if nothing had occurred. Since then I haven't brushed with Nettle caterpillars, even by mistake. And once the new branch started to wilt too I had the good mind of returning the caterpillars to the parent tree.

A notorious number of caterpillars counter the advances of their assailants by giving them itches of varying degrees. That's not something to really worry about, unless one routinely walks into dense foliage, since they all keep to their respective host plants. That is till they start to pupate post summer. The Olepa species is better known as the Darth Maul moth (due to the resemblance of its body's color to the Star Wars antagonist). The caterpillars of this moth launch a massive invasion into our indoors when it is time for them to pupate and are the single biggest non-human nuisance I have faced as a dorm parent at Pathashaala. They feed on the ubiquitous Indian Acalypha (Acalypha indica) which if left to grow in the dormitory courtyard the caterpillars can be a menace for half the year. As soon as these larvae have fed and are fully grown they invade my dormitory in vast hordes, like Roman cohorts. Between August and October is when they reach their peak populations. Very shortly the walls, ceilings and the pillars of the building are blemished with tufts of brown haired larvae gradually growing white cocoons over themselves. And when the moths emerge, they leave behind their furry cocoons super glued to the walls for us to later sit and scrape away. But so far it is only a problem of defacement of school property. Invariably, it will so happen that a caterpillar wandering about on the Wardha tumbler ceiling, looking out for a satisfactory place to metamorphose, will lose its grip exactly when one of the dorm mates are passing below to pick up their laundry or while they are playing Carrom. Soon there will be a vehement knock on my door and a boy is brought to me with an outrageously swollen lip or a cheek, like a plastic surgery gone wrong. Fortunately these swellings don't really hurt and just feel numb but the boys suffer significantly from anticipated pain. At times they don't have a clue of what fell on them and the medical incharge staff immediately puts the student on a vehicle to the hospital. In most scenarios the victim's facial proportions return to normal on the way to the car. Trickier situations arise when some of the boys leave their bureaus open when they leave to school in the mornings and the caterpillars get into their clothes. And I shall refrain from describing whatever ramifications ensued on the rare occasions when a caterpillar walked into an underwear hanging on the clothesline and decided to pupate in the fabric. Co-existence isn't always an easy task.

We teachers here have to deal with similar scenarios when the Jujube bush outside the classroom block bears fruit around the same time of the year. These wild Jujubes are vastly tastier than the ones sold in the markets, but one has to wade through several feet of knee high grass and whatever dwells in it, to get to the fruits. So students are given very stern instructions not to go near the bush and attempt plucking the fruits. But some of the middle school kids always come back from lunch or tea early and fill their pockets with Jujube when the teachers aren't around. A pair of Spotted Munias, which used to be seen nesting on a bifurcation of a branch, soon relocated due to the intermittent lack of privacy every day. But this is also the time when the gray-haired Lappet moth caterpillars, what the kids call Itchy Worms, also gather in large colonies on the trunk of the Jujube and on the termite hills around it to begin their community pupation. Without fail each year a few of the smaller kids while trying to extend their arms to pull down a thorny branch to pluck a fruit and brush a limb on the caterpillar masses. Overtime their tender skins turn from red to redder as they desperately scratch the sores and many later come to the staffroom weeping, albeit claiming not to know the cause for the sudden inflammation. A resident Brainfever bird comes to the tree in the early mornings during these caterpillar gatherings and indulges itself with generous helpings of the larvae. I suppose such birds have itch proof alimentary canals.

There are a motley of other retaliatory and combative behaviors caterpillars exhibit when they perceive a threat. A large number of butterfly and moth larvae may readily empty their bowels on your hand if you attempt to pull them off their leaf or press their abdomens a bit. But apart from that response there are a few other common examples I find quite singular.

When you walk into a Teak plantation keep an eye out for leaves oddly folded and stitched inwards. From the month of August it is likely that every other teak leaf you see will appear this way. This is the work of the Teak Defoliator moth's (Hyblaea puera) larvae, the number one enemy of Teakwood cultivators. Straighten out the leaf and you will find a black and orange caterpillar which instantly stops gnawing on the leaf and shrinks back, considering the prospect that you may probably be a starving Paradise flycatcher. Now if you give it a nudge it will lunge forward and spit out a tar colored liquid on your finger (like a Dilophosaurus from Jurassic park) which I am sure smells and tastes bad, if it isn't downright toxic. If subjected to any more trouble, the critter frantically crawls to the leaf's edge and jumps off and commits suicide. Not really. It hides in the leaf litter for a while and climbs back up again.

By a long shot, the most overtly aggressive caterpillar I have come across is that of the Castor Semi-looper moth (Achaea janata). When it is just out of its egg, the larva is deep purple, which steadily turns paler as it grows till it is light lilac in color at full length. Its actual functional eyes are right above its mouth, but on either side of its head it has large white patches which exactly look like those villainous full white eyeballs lacking any pupils. It feeds from a vast list of unpalatable plants including Castor and some Euphorbia species, and every now and then I find it on a new host plant. Just by itself, the larva is known to be extremely poisonous. And as if that wasn't enough, on either side of its mouthparts it sports two little vampirical tusks. For something as small as a bird, just a close front view of the caterpillar should be enough to horrify it. I wasn't however daunted by its nefarious looks when I came across this caterpillar for the first time. So I picked it up and gave it a few prods on the back, just as I usually do due to my keen interests in discovering new caterpillar defense methods. The creature sprung back immediately and gave a strong bite on the tip of my thumb. It wasn't technically a bite for it had used its tusks to impale my skin but nevertheless. While it attacked me it had also regurgitated some green liquid which were mildly itching the pricks on my finger. I dropped it back on its plant. Its attacks aren't particularly painful but they will suffice to make animals and people give it a wide berth after one unpleasant experience.

HOPES FOR A VANISHING MARSHLAND

THE WEEKEND MORNING IS HERE AND I GET OUT of the auto rickshaw at the turning into the 200 feet road. This is a deafeningly busy road for it is the main commuting lane towards Chennai's thickest IT corridors. Yet it is blinded in its business for its commuters speed past indifferently through the city's largest natural paradise. As I start my walk, just here adjacent to the road right below me, a Grey headed swamphen stalks the floating garbage like a haughty landlord, flicking its tail up now and then, as it looks for morsels. Sandpipers standing on the water's edge however, shake their tails nervously wondering whether they have been spotted or not, whether they should fly away or stay put. Further away in a larger pool, Teals, Garganeys and other migratory ducks are fervently preening themselves while some of them are already out hunting in deeper waters, with their pointy tails pointing to the skies as they wade around upside down, in search of food. The Pallikaranai marshland is now long known to be a dying paradise but nevertheless a paradise in every sense. It is the feeding and breeding grounds for thousands of birds and other fauna. It hosts a diversity of over 110 bird species; a number considerably larger than the number of species found at the famous Vedanthangal bird sanctuary, about eighty kilometers away.

As I walk along the roadside, I see copious volumes of sewage constantly flow through the large cement pipes leading into the marsh from over six surrounding residential areas. One often sees standing at the mouth of these inlets, a heron or an egret, possibly having a strong feeling of reprimand over the desecration of its home. As I walk further I catch sight of Marsh harrier, patiently quartering over the dense marsh reed beds, causing whole flocks of its quarry birds to flee from one end of the marsh to the other. The head of a Purple heron peers out of the reeds like a snake and conceals itself back in again while the more jovial Clamorous Reed Warbler plays peek-a-boo in them, now and then perching on a reed and voicing its crackling call with its beak to the sky. As I approach more open waters I start seeing hundreds of Black winged stilts sitting in dispersed flocks and between the shudders of passing vehicles, one hears the more pleasant clamor of these birds. Closer to the road, Grey headed Lapwings turn over plastic bags caked in sludge, in search of their grubs.

A sewage lorry comes along and parks itself briefly by the roadside. A man gets out and hastily opens a pipe protruding from the sewage tank into the marsh. Quite often, sewage from nearby apartments or IT buildings is emptied here during the earlier morning hours. As one walks further, one comes across mighty hillocks of municipal waste spread over an enormous expanse. Numerous Crows and Black Kites stalk the garbage heaps like rag pickers and fill the skies above. The Crows wait around till a Kite finds itself something edible in a trash mound and then they will chase the bird away and fight over the crumb. This is where most of the garbage from all over the city is dumped and it is its largest landfill. It spans across 250 acres of the wetland and about 4500 tonnes of waste is dumped here daily, as its boundaries increasingly eat into the rest of the water body. In the year of 1970, this dump yard was recorded to be only 19 acres and since then it has grown at such a rate that now it looks like a diseased hill range from afar.

I cross the road, which segments the marsh into two, to the other side. The vast shallow waters on this portion of the wetland host a different diversity of life. Between the months of February and May there is a great deluge of pink on this part of the water body. Hundreds of Greater Flamingos gather here to forage in the shallows, and their swaying necks and clattering beaks overwhelm the waters. It's a pity that most often when a biker pulls over to the road's edge, it is only to relieve himself, completely sightless to the scenery before. Black-Winged Terns and Barn Swallows come in their hundreds too, saturating the air above the wetland with their incessant flight. Near the vegetation, Glossy Ibises glimmer iridescently in their breeding plumage and always appear strikingly handsome. Large flocks of Pelicans and Painted storks congregate on the trees flanking the marsh to one side. My walk ends at the end of this hideous road and I board another auto rickshaw, back home. I turn around to look at the marsh again. At the end of each walk, one goes away with a heart full of reproach for the thousands who race along the wide road so numbly, untouched by the beauty around, blinkered to the flourishing life around.

I remember the times many years back, when as a child I used to travel along the extension of this 200 feet road on the other side of the flyover which now marks the end of the marsh. Back then there was a vast marsh on either side of this road as well, for a very long stretch. It used to be dense with long reeds and I remember being thrilled each time I saw a Pheasant-Tailed Jacana venture out of the vegetation and show its long plumes or when a Tri-colored Munia flew across the road with a ribbon of grass trailing in its bill. I used to peer out to watch the huge Pelicans crossing the skies, grandly flapping their wings and my mother would pull me in, asking me not to extend my head so much outside the vehicle. Today as I travel by this road, tall apartments have taken its place along with hotels and shops with fancy and colorful name boards and the wetland no longer exists. Today when I visit what is left of Pallikaranai, I ask myself and the marsh, with a heavy heart whether several years from now, it too, with all its vast reed beds, the Pelicans, the Flamingos, its placid and fertile waters, would be gone.

Following a PIL filed by residents concerned about the conservation of the wetland, the High Court of Madras rapped the government last year for 'not taking measures for protecting the marsh and for turning a blind eye towards land grabbers and encroachers assisted by politicians and officials.' Justice Kirubakaran, the High Court Judge then, during a hearing stated, "We should protect and preserve nature and the environment, failing which nature's fury would be very dangerous."

Not long after these words were spoken by the Judge, Chennai faced the worst floods in a century, in December of 2015, which took the lives of over 500 people in the city and left over 1000 homeless. Urban planning experts termed this event a 'Manmade disaster' as a result of poor city planning, illegal development and excessive encroachment into water bodies and wetlands which would have otherwise been catchment areas and natural sinks for the rainwater. A trustee of Care Earth Trust, an environmental NGO, stated that the Pallikaranai marsh would have buffered much of the flood's impact on the surrounding areas if it hadn't been so imprudently constructed upon as the marsh has been known as a flood sink for many centuries. The water was left no place to go. Consequently, the residential areas of Thoraipakkam, Pallikaranai, Velachery, Perungudi, Shollinganallur and other adjoining areas near this marshland, were recorded the worst affected places by the flood. As the wetland continued to die in silence, nature gave its gravest wake-up call for its desperate conservation. Just as Krishnamurti once said, 'when one is hurting nature, one is hurting oneself.'

Beauty is the mother of all that which heals, revives and gives larger meaning and purpose. And the lack of beauty is disease, deterioration, death. Now is it not important that we ask ourselves what our relationship is with the birds, with the trees, with the wetlands and with all of life? Do we have a relationship at all? Can beauty exist without relationship, without a fine sensitivity towards people, towards life, towards nature? I believe that we will see this marshland's true indispensable significance to us and to all other life forms if we are someday touched by its beauty. If every other person passing by this marvelous habitat slowed down or stopped and took a few moments to watch the dance of the Flamingos or the quarrelling Swamphens, it would make a tremendous difference to the marshland.

OF BLACKBUCK HERDS

THE VAST EXPANSES OF SCRUBLANDS AND GRASSY plains all across our countryside host a healthy population of Blackbucks. And as summer sets in and the great many rain fed lakes dry up, they proliferate with grasses and the grazing grounds of these antelopes widen as well. Actually in this part of the country, there is no grassland which is apart from a lake. All grasslands become mighty lakes after the monsoons and all the lakes turn into unbounded grasslands with the approach of the warm season. These endemic antelopes tell us an important truth. It is that these seemingly dry and desolate plains sustain their own inimitable diversity and they need to be treasured and protected on par with rainforests. Grasslands are also catchment areas for water during the rains and a buffer during floods. And the aftermath of the Floods of December 2015 is grim testimony to what will result if the larger role of these habitats is neglected and real estate virulently encroaches into them like a rapid skin disease over the landscape. Grasslands are fragile ecosystems, much more fragile than dense impenetrable forests for it is possible for a monstrous bulldozer or a JCB to flatten one overnight and plant into them the foundation stones for the next new apartment complex.

Surrounded by lakes, cultivations and boundless grass fields, Blackbucks are a familiar part of the campus at Pathashaala. Here in South India the male buck has a dark brown coat while its North Indian cousin is jet black. Its trademark, those rugged spiraling horns diverging over its head would have made it appear a fierce beast if it didn't have such benign aspects to its facial features. The does are warm beige colored and their fleet feet and seamless blending with the brazen brown backdrop make up for their lack of horns. These animals are early risers. They are often active before sunrise and one can hear the male's call at the crack of dawn. To me its call sounds quite a like Jungle crow's albeit with a trifle smoother tone. Usually Blackbucks like a large flight range and give people a wide berth. But a lone old male buck can be quite a bold creature as antelopes go and may allow you to sometimes get within thirty feet of it, if you looked away and walked along slowly. A farmer who cultivated vegetables next to a nearby lake used to complain to me about a particular lone buck which used to be a menace to his fields with a particular taste for his Lablab beans. He said it was the oldest buck in the village and lived in solitude like an ascetic who had renounced his matrimonial life. That's what he said. It had the darkest snout, the thickest horns and broad bushy eye brows. A couple of scarecrows near his fence were enough to keep the does away but this one wouldn't consider them at all, and would leap over and raid his farm. It wouldn't even start to run if the man waved his towel and yelled from afar. He too had to jump into his fields and charge at it before the animal felt like snatching its last bite and vacating the premises.

On early summer mornings, a few students, I and Don would go on what we called Blackbuck trails through the vast dry lakebeds. And if Don saw any antelopes before we did, he would get excited and would go on a mad chase behind them till as far as he could. Since none of us could run as fast as either of the animals, we would now shift out attentions towards the birds instead. But once my dog began a pursuit behind a lone male which I believe was the senile animal the farmer had mentioned. It did not seem too daunted by the dog and began a steady gallop away from us. Don ran a bit faster with his tongue flying out of the side of his mouth, but the antelope criss crossed serpentinely through the grass, throwing him off his momentum. Through the misty air one could hear the antelope's hard hooves hitting the dry sun baked ground, like a hammer. The chase had lasted only a few minutes and both animals had reached the tall bund of the lake. Deciding now to end the farce, the Blackbuck stopped abruptly, turned around and lowering its head, it pointed its deeply coiled horns at its pursuer. The dog came to a sliding halt seeing the buck's sudden change of temperament and panted while he took a moment to judge the situation. The male buck swung its head and shook its horns at it again giving one more warning. Now the dog opted for a change of plan, did an about-turn and began a leisurely trot back to rejoin us on the walk.

But usually you will find Blackbucks in herds and they being of a few kinds. A family herd consists of the alpha male, his harem of females and their fawns.

The male is an alert patriarch, always on the lookout, on the guard, watching over the herd and guiding its movements. These herds often enter the campus through the breaches in the fence to graze in the games field. When the children start arriving for the sports period the male spots them coming from quite a distance and watches with an extended neck. Then it stomps its hind legs, signaling the troop to get moving. Some adamant youngsters still continue to chomp on the grass and the male loses patience and swings its formidable horns at them, at which they would lift up their necks and now trot along to the fence without further ado. And what I have found most incredible about the male is that most often it waits aside and lets its entire herd cross over to the other side (probably even taking a head count) and then is the last one to exit the fence.

Then you will come across the all female herd, the most vigilant of all, with every doe on its guard, their ears and stubby tails quivering to the smallest sound and ready to flee at the drop of a hat. I suppose they are a group of girls hanging around together, yet to be wooed by a worthy male. When a threat is sensed, one of the females leap into the air on both feet like a bouncing spring and the whole camp follows cue and absconds. I have time and again been surprised at the vigilance of these female herds. While wading through coarse shoulder high Andropogon grass down a lake bed, all of a sudden some hundred feet away, a group of females, which for all this while had been sitting in the grass, would sense my coming, stand up, peer in my direction and take to their heels. There was no way they could have caught a glimpse of me through the sheer density of the grass while they sat amidst it. They couldn't have heard me or my footsteps for the winds and the grating rustle of the grasses are too loud. And I don't want to think that they could have smelt me.

The other kind of herd you will chance upon is the bachelor herd, consisting of one grown alpha male always accompanied along by another sub adult male. These pairs, of an experienced adult and an apprentice, are frequently found. The younger one is yet to acquire the dark brown pelage of maturity and its horns are still short little prongs. It follows around its senior, learns the lay of the land, learns where the lushest pastures lie, where its community's territories end and where to run to and take cover when in danger. The older male exercises firm control over the younger one, and will use its horns if it needs to keep it in line. I once came across such a bachelor duo grazing just beyond the campus fence. I lay down on my belly and began crawling forward, grabbing clumps of grass for leverage. There was a trench freshly dug up adjacent to the fence for water drainage and if I could covertly slip myself into it, I could watch the animals close at hand, with my head barely peeping out and without scaring them away. As I moved along in this inch worm fashion, I stopped dead each time one of the Blackbucks raised their heads between munching on grass to scrutinize this strange creature creeping towards them. I was able to reach the trench without making the animals too nervous and I rolled into an algae ridden stagnant stretch of rainwater. My camera got caked in thick slush and required serious servicing. The older male now walked a few steps forward to see what the splash was about. I crouched inside with only the upper half of my head visible to the antelope. It decided that it was time that it and its companion left the place and anyways it was close to dusk. It turned to its companion and stomped its legs a couple of times, and swung its head. Junior seemed least interested in leaving and turned its back to it and continued nibbling on grass. The adult male was in no mood to entertain any disobedience and butted the younger one to the ground and rolled it over with its horns. After this, junior was more than willing to join its companion and both of them began to walk away towards the scrubland further beyond.

WINGS IN THE SKIES

FROM THE MONTH OF JULY, THE WESTERN COAST of India starts receiving its dose of the monsoons. To escape these torrential rains, thousands and thousands of butterflies from the Western Ghats migrate eastwards to the plains. Everywhere else in the world it is largely the hostile winters which drive all the animal migration making them travel down along the longitudes to warmer and tropical regions, but here these butterflies flutter along over latitudes across the peninsula to less wetter regions, driven by the unique pattern of rains we face in our Subcontinent. This migration is a grand spectacle and for many weeks, from a few feet from the ground till as high as the eye can resolve, the skies are saturated with butterflies. Those with smaller wings and erratic flight like the Emigrants, Limes, Jays and the little Blues fly low, often in large swarms by the coasts, to be carried by the winds, but broad winged and powerful fliers like the Blue tigers, Crows and the Roses soar and sail at much greater heights, higher than the circling Black kites, deep beyond the dark rain clouds and far beyond what my binoculars can bring to my view. This is a season where there are ten butterflies to every flower and even a traffic policeman standing amidst a deafening lane cannot help stealing a glimpse at an Emigrant prancing past his gaze.

These plains in the Eastern strip of the peninsula are the nurseries for the offspring of these butterflies and were also their own, half a year back. As soon as the insects settle here, before they can acclimatize or get accustomed to the new habitat, courting and wooing amongst them, begins. The males first look around for their aphrodisiacs and the salts which make them potent in the first place. They gather on the moist banks of ponds, lakes, rivers and streams in large numbers and insert their proboscises like bendable straws into the sand to draw in the salts they are after. But in contemporary times, butterflies have found themselves a hundred other alternatives. The soggy and drenched mud around an overflowing sewage tank for instance the males find downright irresistible. The wet mixture of cement, sand and gravel dissolved by the rain and imbibed by the soil, around a construction site too is a patch the migrant males like to mud-puddle in. Or just on puddle ridden, gravel topped walkways, plenty of males may gather on. And similarly fresh drenched compost from a compost pit.

The Blues primarily, adore cow dung and I frequently borrow some from the campus bulls, mix them with some water or if they are wet enough, I strew them around just as they are, in the mornings. Then I come after lunch or so and find the pat teaming with Line blues, Grass jewels and Grass blues. And on our walks, Don likes to take a leak by the roadside and on our way back, we find clumps of butterflies on many of his spots.

The Indian Heliotrope (Heliotropium indicum) is a plant which has long inflorescences like elephant trunks and it is something which too attracts butterflies, like it has cast a spell, when it is dead and rotting. Especially the male Tigers and Crows. Other than that you can take a pair of shears and chop the tops of a patch of Crotalaria plants and butterflies will come to the oozing phloem like ants to sugar solution.

August noon…
the company of butterflies
as I cycle

Courting begins simultaneously, for both the migrants and the residents. Now a butterfly you may have erstwhile known as a shy and diffident specimen may become a creature of great nerve and valor when it is wooing a female. The best instance I can recount for this was when a Common Blue bottle was skipping behind a female asking for its hand, round and round a large Cinnamon tree. Then the chase went around a Rose apple tree, where female would attend to the fresh white blossoms while the male sat on a leaf nearby pleading for its acceptance, like cheesy Orlando to Rosalind. It had managed to mob away a couple of other males who tried intercepting its chances, which makes sense, but then suddenly overhead passed a Jungle crow which infuriated the Bottle further. It gave the bird a lengthy chase close at its heels and I am sure the Crow never noticed the insect tailing it for all that while for then, although Crows are not quite fond of eating butterflies, it is likely that it may have taken a chunk out of its wing.

Various kinds of courtship chases exist in butterflies. The Jays, Emigrants and the Albatrosses go on marathons behind their respective females from one horizon to the other and these chases happen faster than the fastest I can run with a camera beating on my chest. Often three or more males fly behind a single Emigrant female and when the exhausted thing perches on a flower for a drink, invariably all its pursuers bump into it and topple it over. The Jezebels take things a bit slower and one can walk or jog behind a courting pair, but you would have to drown in lakes and shatter from hills if you ever wanted to keep up with them all through. The Tigers, Roses and the Mormons however do a slow wooing flutter close behind their desired mates, always keeping within your garden compound or even a small patch in it.

Dapper little Pierrots go after eachother in high speed revolutions about a small radius close to the ground, with a frequency of three or four circles per second. Then both butterflies sit down on the ground for a while, possibly to let their rapidly spinning heads become still on their neck joints again. And then again they go on dizzying circles seeing which one cannot be sure whether it is the male which is behind the female or whether it is vice-versa. The Wanderers weave through tall and dense vegetation at a leisurely pace, playing hide and seek. And then there is the strange case of the Lemon pansies and the Evening browns, wherein the male would be in gentle pursuit of the slow flying female criss-crossing through the grass. Then suddenly once in a while the female would rise twenty feet straight into the air and then plummet down again to the ground, like it had just hit a passing thermal and the male would have to do the same if it wanted to stay in pursuit. Whatever is the attribute the female tests the male for by bounding up and down like this, in fits.

A male psyche on the other hand pursues its girl so very very slowly, and both drift along like large flakes of snow in the air as if tethered together by some unseen cord. The Psyche is most known for its slow meandering flight, so much so that you can easily count the number of times it flaps as it saunters about. But it is yet more renowned for being an incessant flier, feeding your hopes but never fulfilling them, making you pray to God that it should perch sometime soon. And once you disturb a resting Psyche, you will grow a beard before it sits again.

There is a grove of Madras thorn trees (Pithecellobium dulce) in the Southwestern corner of Pathashaala's campus which has about two dozen mature trees in it. Their canopies interlock with eachother, leaving only thin mottled sunshine to touch the floor. Soft tender grass grows here interlaced with Asparagus vines and one would be tempted to fall, roll and cuddle on the ground, if not for the piles of thorny branches shed by these trees over many years. This time of the year the Common Lineblues and the Tail-less Lineblues swarm around here, for these trees are the host plants for their larvae. These are little non-descript butterflies with dull under wings with a whole lot of lines on them. The males have deep purple upper sides but those too are dull in the females. And to procure a mate, all the males loop around the crowns of the trees behind the females, in every orientation and angle, all at once, with intangible speed, that they could very well model electrons going around in their orbitals.

But the courting chase which fascinates me the most is that of the Common Crow. It is among the most persistent of all male butterflies. It wields a yellow brush (androconium) coming out of its posterior using which it is supposed to release pheromones into the territory it occupies to catch the fancy of the opposite sex. I suppose this stuff smells like expensive cologne to the females. Once the male crow sights a prospective mate it flies to it and keeps close, within a foot of it. Now even if you regularly took walks, say several times a day, you will see dozens of these courting crows but only once in several days will you see a female actually comply after a chase and then mating ensuing. I have never counted though, but probably ninety percent or more of these chases end in rejection. Many frail hearted males you may see give up as soon as they start but others endure for very long. It is a tedious chase and the male crow tries everything in its power to subdue the hard to catch female. Now and then, when a male crow is close enough, it may butt headlong onto the female to throw it off its course. When the female sits for a brief respite, it does so with its hind wings covering its abdomen so that the male doesn't make any attempts. But what the male does do now is hover over it with a fierce rapidity, creating a little wind with its wings, making leaves and twigs quiver, and capable of blowing away the perched butterfly if it didn't sit tight. It wants to keep the female constantly on the wing so that it gets exhausted soon.

Now during this whole affair no opportunists are tolerated in the least. Any butterfly, even if it is from a different species with no intentions ever to interbreed, which comes close to the female which is being pursued, is bombarded and chased away by the male. But if it so happens that another male crow comes by with plans for the same lady, then an airborne battle breaks out and both males clash and swirl till there is an undoubted victor. The female often takes advantage of this window of time and flies deep into vegetation or hides under foliage. Now what really works out between a pair of butterflies when they decide to mate? I have wondered. Most often the females seem downright petrified when they are doggedly chased and harassed by males. I am sure there exist some other lepidopteran nuances of courtship, which maybe completely invisible and incomprehensible to us, but those which are gentler, more tactful and which work better than mere hounding.

The paranoid nature of the male crow goes to great extents. There have been times when I have walked too close to it or the female it is behind, and it has turned around and flown straight to my chest and head- butted me, taking me for a rival. I confess I had no intentions whatsoever of appropriating any of its prospects.

The Crow seeks the Oleander to lay its eggs and let its progeny grow on. The caterpillars of the Oleander Hawk moth with their ghoulish eye spots feed on the Oleander too and the Gardenia plants. There is not a plant you can find in September which doesn't host caterpillars. The brilliant Laburnums, on each of their leaves will have a caterpillar of an Emigrant, hiding along the midribs. The Indian Beech tree will have the larvae of the Ceruleans, Sunbeams, Death head moths, and numerous others, neatly chomping away its leaves from the tip to the stalk. Unlike bugs, caterpillars do a thorough job of eating leaves. A bug will drill slipshod cheese holes here and there randomly on a leaf and then fly off to a different one, but the caterpillar can't afford to do that for it has no wings yet and hence runs the risk of falling off. The Limes and Mormons, scourge the Lime plants, Bel plants and the Curry leaves and the Blue tiger larvae are most fond of Green Milkweed Creepers (Wattakaka volubilis).

The parent butterflies are known to spend what little is left of their lives, here in the plains. But their offspring migrate back to the Western Ghats just in time to escape the relentless November–December rains here. Again the skies suffuse with these insects, from the floor right till the heavens, this time much brighter in color for these butterflies have just only freshly emerged before they begin their long journey to the hills.

A saint once said that paradise is not a place but a state of consciousness. And so many are the souls who have known all there is to be known and learned all there is to be learnt from a single tree or a forest, in exile, banished or shut away from the world outside. For there exists no real world outside but only the glow of perception from within, giving meaning, permitting creation, allowing existence. And likewise, what makes the land around beautiful beyond words and what makes life around the most glorious event to witness is not a hundred thousand butterflies flooding the skies, like fragments from a rainbow. What makes heaven on earth are the wide reverential eyes, watching them breathlessly.

THE DRAMA OF KUKRIS

I WAS ON A LONG WALK ONE EARLY MORNING
during the summer holidays, down the road by the
village lake. The sharp whiff of burnt grass and Babul
trunks from the lake, wet by the slight mist made me
think of the fire a few days back. I walked into the little
settlement of huts where the metalled road became
large blocks of partially buried stones. A family of
three stood outside their hut looking panicked. The
man of the house searched the vegetation outside for
a Casuarina log and picked up one which was about
his size, while his wife and the mother of either one
stood watching. I felt eager to give the snake which
had entered their home, a turn of fate. It had probably
gone in during the night and was discovered just then.
The elderly woman cautioned me that it was a Cobra
which had gotten inside and to be careful. So I myself
felt cautious and picked up a much smaller stick which
was for aiding me to lead the snake out. My eyes took
a few moments to adjust to only the thin sliver of light
in the hut and then right away, curled under an earthen
pot I found a Russell's Kukri. It was a snake which fit
comfortably in my palm. However I also looked around
for the Cobra but didn't find one. The Russell's Kukris
have an archaic inverted 'W' on their necks which when
coupled with the terror of snakes, were enough for it
to be misidentified as a Spectacled Cobra. But I, living

between concrete walls with a proper roof over my head, living in affluence in every aspect, can go on and on about how these rustics don't understand snakes at all and nor did they even care to. Affluence is a poison to empathy. This man was truly afraid for his wife and mother and was least interested in snake taxonomy. He could only feel grateful the snake was removed from his house before anything undue occurred. I let the snake go in the vegetation closeby and resumed my walk.

But Kukris are among the most docile and harmless snakes. And I speak for the Russell's Kukri and the Banded Kukri, which are the most common and widespread of them (I read that there happens to be a White barred Kukri in the Northeastern hills of India which gets furious when handled and inflicts painful bites.) All Kukris come with a brand on themselves. Like the Russells' 'W,' the Banded Kukri has a chevron mark on its neck followed by black bands all along its body. Now one of the Tamil names for the venomous Common Krait is *Kattuviriyan* which can be loosely translated to 'Banded snake.' Most of the village folks take the name quite literally and I have come across many people who have pointed to a passing Kukri with an aghast expression and clutch their children closer to them. All that has bands isn't a Krait!

These two Kukris never bite as a rule. Except once, I had just manually cleaned out the drain pipe of my dorm's sink which was clogged by a whole family of aestivating Ornate Narrow Mouthed Frogs. And immediately later I picked up a Banded Kukri which had entered the Common room and the snake tried swallowing my pointer in earnest, because my finger enticingly smelt of frogs to it. But that apart, what they lack in tooth and claw, the Kukris very well make up for in their antics. When cornered, a Kukri will put on an extraordinarily convincing act of ferocity, without the slightest shade of doubt or diffidence. The Banded Kukri will jump into a sidewinder's pose, like a Saw scaled viper, and make lightning fast forward lunges. But if you saw through its pretence and watched closely, you would note that it strikes with its mouth shut.

A Russell's will put on an act with greater self confidence and will come out of the way to taunt its opponent and make its point. Once I found an adult Russell's Kukri, one about a foot long, an afternoon shedding its old skin in a crevice of an open brick wall. Its lips had just split and its papery old skin was coming over its nostrils. I ran back and returned with my camera, to take a video of the whole process and show the students later. In a few minutes it had gradually moved along the brickwork and pulled away its skin till its neck. And then it froze, like it had just seen something which was not to be seen. I was sweating profusely and the snake must have caught a whiff of me. Its newly uncovered nostrils were probably enhanced in their faculties. Or it must have just sensed that it is being intently watched. Its tongue flickered in and out suspiciously. I slowly brought my knees to rest on the ground as I could squat on my toes for only so long. This caught the attention of the creature and infuriated it. It slid down the wall onto the cement plinth, retracted its fore body and struck out at me repeatedly. It moved closer and closer and lunged at me till it was banging its mouth on my knee. Its jaws were shut however and it had no intentions to bite but I should say it was a remarkable bluff. "Trust me, I too am dangerous" was the snake's heated assertion. Then my unresponsiveness to its emphatic drama seemed to put it off a bit, and with an air of dissatisfaction, it slid away on the plinth around the corner of the building, I presume to continue its ecdysis in privacy.

These snakes are creatures of the night like most of the others. Only on cold mornings during the monsoons, when they really could use some warmth do they come out to bask on the plinths and the sidewalks at daybreak. Some years back the renovation of the dining hall was happening at Pathashaala. A dividing wall had to be knocked down to reshape the interior space of the kitchen area. Men with sledge hammers started their work some hours before noon. Not long after, the supervisor called me for help. Not that he lacked any man power, He said the wall was filled with snakes and his men were refusing to carry on with the job. I was there in a jiffy, dropping all my other errands. Surely enough, with each knock, as the bricks crumbled and dribbled down to the floor, a snake would jump out of a crevice from within. Here was another revelation of a long held mystery to me. A wall with cracks of width enough for them to crawl in was among the places these creatures vanish during the drier months and hibernate in. Just sometime back I had been digging up dry crab holes outside my room, just as one of those things you do as a matter of interest. I happened to find a Striped Keelback hibernating inside one, in the damp clay right at the end. This too is a snake which goes totally absent during the rest of the year but then abruptly appears in on the scene after the rains. They are ubiquitous infact after the very first rains and I have always wondered where so many of them had been hiding. I had found two hiding places, walls for the Kukris and Crab holes for the Striped Keelbacks. Some Wolf snakes too jumped out of the brickwork now and then but they were almost all Kukris. On my reassurance and more due to the supervisor's hasty insistence, the demolition reluctantly continued. I put the snakes in a laundry bag and released them batch by batch in the prostrate undergrowth nearby. Some of them jumped out of the fissures and absconded into the rubble heap on the floor. Once in a while a Kukri would land in front of a worker and put on its act of aggression and the horrified man would drop his tools and scamper. After a break for lunch I sat there till late afternoon, till the work for the day was over. I would have bagged and released about two dozen snakes that day. More got away by themselves. But I am sure that as the night fell, all the snakes searched for some other part of the building, found a crack in the wall and climbed in again.

OF THE MILKWEED COMMUNITY

THROW IT IN THE MOST DERELICT CORNER OF THE town, in the most utterly impoverished conditions you can find where few plants have managed to even barely sprout, and the Giant Milkweed will grow forth royally. From right within a landfill, or beside the stench of an open sewer, through the dilapidated ruins of broken brick and concrete, amidst the blue-metal stones by railway tracks or from a crevice on a compound wall, there are a few places this Milkweed is unwilling to rise from. Its grit and versatility is inspiring, yet it survives not by propagating itself rapaciously, dominating over all the other vegetation. Species with such tendencies quickly meet with the axe or the JCB's arm, the very plight the Prosopis thorn is facing right now. The Milkweed instead exists in abundance together with all the other plants, never seeking to take over the land for itself. Therefore it lives and thrives.

The latex which flows through the milkweed's stems is well known to be highly poisonous, but that's only to our stomachs and to cattle and other grazing mammals. A number of animals have adapted to feed exclusively on this plant and live off it. And as a bonus they render themselves unpalatable to their predators as well! The caterpillars of the Plain Tiger butterfly, clad in Zebra stripes, almost solely feed on the Milkweeds, leaf, stem, flower and all, and hence go untouched by birds. I am sure that the major reason for this butterfly being amongst our most common ones is due to the widespread abundance of its host plant. Moreover the plant's perennial nature allows this insect to breed and be seen throughout the year.

Its sap gives the Milkweed another line of defense apart from making it poisonous. Several are the times while playing cricket in the streets, when I have jumped into a clump of Milkweeds, in a feat of heroic fielding. And on being smeared with its milk in many places, I won't forget how on those days I itched and scratched myself blue.

As we enter May, the summer is climbing to its apex and the Giant Milkweeds begin growing their seed pods. They are shaped just like eyeballs in their orbits and I am tempted to draw on them pupils using glow paint. I am guessing that it's Tamil name Erukkan, which translates to bull's eye, refers to this resemblance. When the seed pods mature they split open with the Sun's heat and from the mouth of each follicle flat brown seeds drift into the air, carried by glistening white silken strands of hair. Wind and fate are twin siblings. And to allow oneself be carried by either one without a shard of resistance, undaunted by the uncertainty of each gust and letting go, letting be is among the loftiest ideals any entity can reach. I hear these little seeds whispering to the wind "carry me to wherever you may go, however far away and foreign and I will grow." Red Milkweed Beetles now congregate just at the openings of these pods to catch the outgoing seeds, the only edible things the plant produces. When I think of Summer I think of ripe mangoes, of tall heaps of tender coconuts and succulent palm fruits. I think of long afternoon naps and of the dry hot rising air making whole landscapes quiver. I think of limes, fish, chilies, garlic and other pickled condiments on large white cloths being dried on the terraces. And I think of countless white Milkweed seeds floating in the atmosphere, appearing and disappearing in the intense sunrays, like those obscure filaments we see drifting within our eyes. At these times of the year I keep my balcony doors shut at home, especially at lunch as only a slight breeze would be enough to garnish all the dishes on the table with Milkweed hair.

In the city, the soil seems like a dead substance mixed with all manner of filth. But I am reminded each year of all the worlds I overlook, all the realities I name, label and forget about, when the nymphs of the Painted Grasshoppers crawl out from the mud. They crawl up from beneath the discarded plastic heaps, from beneath cement rubble, stone and tar, from under the faeces of man, dog and cattle. Their overwintering eggs have been hatched by the heat of the solsticing sun after almost a whole year after they have been laid and buried by the parent Grasshoppers. These nymphs emerge in their thousands and climb on to the closest Milkweed plants to which their feeding loyalties exclusively lie with. But their presence goes largely unnoticed due to their speckled and dirty green complexion. They start taking on the younger and tender leaves first, competing with the Plain Tiger caterpillars and you can see them grow by the day. If you grab one from a leaf, it will shoot at your hand, extra refined poisons it has accumulated from the plant, from squirters all along its back, a liquid so noxious and nauseating that you will never want to smell it a second time in your life. But inspite of this, now and then I do see a Warbler or a Bulbul hover by a Milkweed and take away a nymph. A poison by definition only begins its work when it is ingested. So it is recommended that you wash your hands well after your investigations with these critters.

In the weeks to follow the nymphs begin to develop wings and grow into Grasshoppers. This new creature, in stark incongruity with its juvenile form, looks like something out of a Children's coloring book. It is now dressed in gaudy green stripes, deep red wing tips and glaring alternations of blue and yellow on its head and limbs, so conspicuous and eye catchy that I wouldn't cross a road with this insect in direct view. These blaring colours are warning boards to hungry birds, cautioning them to take a chunk out of their toxin laden bodies at their own grave risk. But why does the grasshopper choose to blend with the leaves during its younger stages? Is it because it accumulates the plant's poisons over time and only as an adult is its toxicity most formidable? Or is it that its colours also serve to attract mates? Or could it be that since now it has wings it can be showy as well and manage to fly away in the face of real danger? It could be that the reason is all these at once and more. But even an adult grasshopper takes precautions when it decides to take out a thick fully grown Milkweed leaf. It first walks to its petiole near the stem and gnaws on it a bit and waits till some of the toxic milk spills out of its veins. Only then does it come over to the leaf and begin to nibble on it.

The flowers of the Giant Milkweed are subtly purple, the color you can rest your eyes on. They hold manifold symmetries within their star shaped petals and elicit more and more fascination when you look into one, as you twirl it between your fingers. Its fragrance is not meant to entice our senses but to specifically woo Carpenter bees (Xylocopa species). For these bees, Milkweed flowers are their single most favorite. Its extraordinary to think that the deadly plant, the touch of whose sap can cause cataracts in any creature's eyes and a teaspoon full can kill goats, has its sweet and nectarine aspect too, accessible only to a few creatures which help it pollinate and procreate. Ants and a handful of butterflies attend these flowers as well. So do Sunbirds and White-eyes and a few other birds which are fond of nectar. But the most allegiant to this flower is the Carpenter Bee which lugs itself from stigma to stigma; its wings humming a monotone, barely able to carry its clumsy body dangling below. And as it decides and settles on a flower it is blown away by passing vehicles and knocked over by the wind many a time. When it finally lands on a flower it tumbles and slides on the petals before it can crawl up and get a grip to draw in the nectar. I believe there is a myth that according to the laws of aerodynamics, a bee by its shape and gait shouldn't be able to fly in the first place. Well evidently this is atleast partially true with this bee.

Soon we would have fought our wars, fired our missiles and brought about our hasty demise before long, on our age old tryst in seeking absolute power over our own species and over the planet. And along with the debris and the bombshells, our bones and skulls too will litter the land masses, as our only legacy. But probably for those who are content with the few comforts they have and are grateful for the little space they have been blessed with on Earth, for those who coexist as a way of life, like a Milkweed community, Life may deem them fit too to live beyond.

FRANCOLIN CALLS

THE CRACK OF DAWN IS ANNOUNCED MORE promptly and vociferously by the Francolins than the proverbial Roosters. My room at Pathashaala was in the southern corner of the campus, during my high schooling. The vast field of grass behind my room would abound with these stout birds, scurrying here and there like large humpty dumpty eggs with legs, along trains of twitching grass. In summer, when the grasses dried up and crumbled to mud, with only their hard dormant shoots protruding like thick thorns from the ground, a Francolin's feathers would still be seamlessly merged with the land's texture and brazen shade. With the first light, these birds would voice their piercing calls from right beneath my window, punishing me if I ever chose to rise late. For a while I remember wearing cotton buds in the night to guard myself against the cold morning mist and also the Francolin's morning yells. But if the bird ever failed at this, the five horse power water pump behind my room, which would be switched on around half past six every morning, would certainly get me out of bed. *Be-careful Be-careful Be-careful,* their calls would distinctly sound like to me. One bird would begin and some distance away, another bird would respond in the same fashion and then one more from somewhere across the land, and like this each day, as dawn came and dusk settled, the little community of these ground dwelling birds would commune and announce their whereabouts to eachother. I recollect Hume's untypical impression on the Francolin, which were then and still, called Partridges. He says "They run very swiftly and gracefully, they seem to glide rather than run, and a native lover can pay no higher compliment to his mistress than to liken her gait to that of a partridge." The native lover's mistress would have been slightly less pleased if her voice and wake-up call as well were likened to that of a Francolin.

Through the stainless steel mesh window, I could clandestinely observe the entire wilderness behind my room without being noticed, for the metal reflecting light on the outer side renders the inner contents of the room invisible. I could see Hares nibbling on grass, with their ever vigilant ears and twitching noses. I could see Jackal mothers trotting along with their pups, which would jump up and catch falling raindrops in their little snouts. And after the rains, Ducks, Sandpipers and Open-billed storks, entire flocks of them, would stand there in the flooded land, sometimes within an arm's reach as the steel mesh had its veil over me. But for most of the year, from within my room, I watched my Francolin neighbors for this was their beat. To the outside world, they would take all precautions to not be spotted. One would point its beak to the skies and voice its call and its larynx would bounce up and down along its long throat. Immediately later the bird would crouch forward and sprint several poles away, as if it didn't want its call traced back to its location. It would call again and do the same. If anything passed closeby, and the Francolin was sure that it hadn't been spotted yet, then it will bend forward and bury itself in the vegetation, but with its eye watching sideways.

Now the most startling and unpleasant surprise which one can be ever subjected to, other than when a clump of large, hard, rotting palm fruits falls off a tree and lands on one's head, is when one unwittingly walks too near a hiding Francolin. From right beneath your feet will burst forth a loud explosion of wing beats, making you jump, choke and hold your beating heart from pouncing out of its cavity, while the bird flies away to its safety. And before you can take another breath, look around and understand what had just transpired, its mate will take off a few yards away from where the other surfaced from.

After a hearty lunch, it is impossible for me to trudge along with the day without taking an afternoon nap. Especially in the summers, I have to aestivate for a couple of hours when the sun is at its apex, if my brain is to start cooperating with me again. If nothing, I take a short snooze over my desk. On many summer evenings, during the holidays, I have abruptly woken up in my room amidst a strange haze, coughing up dust seeping in through my window. Pushing aside my curtains fully, I would discover a pair of Francolins enjoying a mud bath. The gravel on the path to my dormitory is particularly powdery and these birds loved this spot. They would vigorously rub their bellies on the grit and then tilt over on every side and scrub their wings, necks and foreheads. They end up scrubbing each other's feathers as well as they jiggle around.

The only thing they don't do is to roll over and wiggle their backs on the ground. A copious quantity of fine dust, like clear soot from a chimney, is thrown up in clouds during these long episodes of grooming. And when they are done, they leave behind two large and strange, oval depressions on the walkway, for people to look at and wonder.

It is also in summer that the Francolins decide to have their chicks. Four or five little miniatures following their parents as they all cross the road, is a common sight in our countryside. Like a duck protects its ducklings, the Francolin too will put itself in danger's path to keeps its babies safe. I remember a walk I was taking around the Hadosiddapura Lake in Bangalore some months back. An adult Francolin emerged from the vegetation and walked right into my path some distance away, as if by purpose, and eyed me with its neck held as erect as possible. My camera was around my neck and I silently strode behind the bird as it kept dashing ahead like a Roadrunner, along the curved path. I was lured by its open presence and the prospect of a clear shot, but what was notable was that it kept stopping now and then between its bursts of running and looked behind, as if to make sure I was following. And I kept following it. At this point, from some distance behind me, from where this bird had emerged from, came the sound of familiar heavy wing beats along with some more subdued ones. Another adult, its mate I am sure, was on its way to a Babul tree far away, along with four of its chicks at its heels. Now seeing its family safe, this one abandoned me and took off as well and rejoined with them in the vegetation under the tree.

RESIDING WITH SIGNATURE SPIDERS

NEITHER IN IMPENETRABLE FORESTS NOR IN an urban concretized setting, but in all the habitats which occur in the midway thrive the Signature spiders (Argiope sp). It is known by a number of names. Signature spider, Speckled banded Four-leg and Giant cross spider are some. Once I was told by someone that it is also called the St. Andrews spider because of the way the spider held pairs of its legs together which made it look like the Holy cross the saint held in his hand (his cross wasn't very different from the crosses held by any of the other apostles though). The spider in its range puts up its web, like a bunker shop, in any vacant space left for it to find. Vertices in and around buildings, within alcoves, windows, table legs, plants in your garden especially if they flower, bifurcations on branches and stretched across two paddy plants in a paddy cultivation are among places that you are sure to find them. I have found several of them using my clothes lines as grapples to erect their webs while I am off on a field trip and occasionally across my cycle's handlebars if I have left it parked without using it for a few days.

Like all the other orb web spiders which have chosen to live a life of patience and resignation, which don't seek out their prey but entrust life to bring them their daily insect to their lairs, this one too sits upside down right at the centre of its large web. On a black and pentagonal abdomen, the spider sports chalk white and yellow bands, giving it not a tinge of concealment or camouflage. Their characteristic color and silhouette is unmistakable even from a distance. On a closer look you will notice two red chelicerae protruding from either side of its mouth like the sinister teeth of a bloodthirsty vampire which the creature rightly uses to grab and devour its prey. Where they rest their legs, these spiders make themselves four fancy foot cushions of sorts, a thick zig-zag web lace or stabilimenta, a special amenity which has reminded some naturalist of an illegible autograph, quite likely his doctor's, and hence started calling them Signature spiders. A few smaller members of the Argiope genus stitch for themselves a different kind of stabilimentum, one consisting of wavy concentric circles, which are not just foot rests but an entire seat for them. Now why do these arachnids build for themselves these sturdy footholds? And also why do they hold their legs in pairs and not all eight splayed out like any other spider? Is it to look less like a spider to flies flying by? On some hot windy days the wind blows in swift spurts and the spider's web oscillates dangerously to and fro. When the draughts are strong enough to rip the web's grapples from the wall or the branch, I have seen this spider catch the firmer zigzag webbing and shake its whole web back and forth, out of phase with the wind, making both amplitudes cancel out and hence save its house. I also think that in a similar manner it shakes off dead rotting insect carapaces from the strands of its web which it has already sucked out dry.

Observing a spider requires a level of patience, equal to the magnitude of that of the spider itself. One hardly sees it budge from its location throughout the day. But when an ill fated insect is intercepted by its mortal threads, then the spider bursts alive and shows surprising activity, scampering to its prey and parceling it in its sticky web for consuming right away or storing it in a corner for later. When the day gets hot you may find the creature languidly move to a shady corner only to resume its repose.

During the routine cleaning of the Pathashaala campus just before the school term begins, all the galleries of spider webs and cob webs are cleared from the buildings using long dusting brooms, the length of two or three men, along with all the other dusting and the washing of the place. So just before this cleaning spree I used to gather the Signature spiders from the assembly hall from every pillar and wall corner and let them loose in the long hall of the staff residence, which was at that time the room provided for me. I intended to acquaint myself better with these arachnids. Within a couple of days some would have finished constructing their webs on the wall corners, windows and on the pillars in the verandah. Most would have however decamped elsewhere, not happy with their new location. Inevitably, one or the other of the staff working in the campus would notice these novel decorations in my room and get them cleared in my absence. But in the meantime I have been able to make some naïve investigations to understand the ways of these creatures. My methods were as inane as they can be but I did uncover some interesting aspects of the Signature spider's behavior.

When I disturb these cold faced spiders by prodding them with my finger, they showcase some tactics of evasion appropriate to the magnitude of pestering they are subjected to. When I touched a spider on its back it would cling tight to its web and vibrate it with all its might, like it is being electrocuted; continuing for a while even after the disturbance has stopped. I suppose it is making itself difficult to catch or peck. At times it decides to slip right into the centre of the web, through the slender apertures of the strands and perch itself on the other side, where it may find more peace. Go to the other side and prod it and it will slip back through again to this side. Otherwise it may scurry away and crouch on one corner. If it finds the pestering to be too persistent then it drops to the ground on a thread line and waits in hiding, sometimes acting dead. Most often it will later climb back up again. But I have seen some abandon that web altogether and build a new one in someplace else where it thinks it has a greater chance to be left alone, peacefully in its meditative existence.

There is another interesting phenomenon I discovered when I meddled further. A Signature spider never spent a fraction of a moment on another's web when it was introduced onto one. As soon as the creature's feet touched a conspecific's web, with a strong air of abhorrence, it immediately dropped down and scurried away.

Entertaining my curiosities further, I wanted to find out how the spiders would react to mock prey which was ensnared by its web. I made several fly sized tissue paper balls and one by one tossed them on a spider web, on the extremities. The spider's responses were quite intriguing. If a tissue ball just silently got stuck, like a dart on a dartboard, then the spider wouldn't turn its attention. But if the tissue ball tumbled down a bit before getting stuck, then the spider would instantly charge towards it. However it does come to realize that it tried to paralyze an already inanimate object either when it is close to it or as soon as it begins to wrap it up, after which it will return despondently to its perch again. So clearly the spider's stimulus for action was the presence of struggle on the web, not just a brief jerk. Probably this is how it distinguishes between a trapped fly wrestling to break free and a stuck piece of debris or dry leaf litter carried by the wind. And thus it makes sure it expends its energies only towards profitable prospects.

Watching a spider on its web routinely on your wall corner can begin to turn your eyes alchemical as it sees the rest of the world. We in our contemporary ways of living have learnt to only respond to gross sensations and hard stimuli, to advertisements, to money, to pain, to power, to gunshots and to death and the many subtle and subliminal worlds of feeling, of sensations and of experience are far beyond the purview of what we call our lives. Now watch a spider every day on its web sharing your room, its stillness will acquire meaning, its silence will speak to you and its slightest movements will be dramatic events and so will you begin to be touched by life's slightest gestures.

FISHERFOLK OF THE CULVERTS

AFTER THE RELENTLESS RAINS IN DECEMBER which is often accompanied by a raging cyclone, all the village lakes around Pathashaala would fill up to the brim and flow over. For the next couple of months none of the crop fields need irrigation and for several days whole landscapes of verdant grass would remain inclined along the water's flow. The two canals cutting through the campus would run full as well and breach their banks, as they gush through the two massive cement culverts conveying the water from one side to the other. For some years there lived two Checkered Keelback snakes around one canal, one large adult and a slender juvenile. During the hotter months they would hardly be seen, and if at all you did, you would see them prowling only in the dead of the night. After the monsoon rains however these snakes would be active throughout the day. Their heads would be floating just above the surface, soaking in the warmth of daylight, of a well or a stagnant pool and would momentarily vanish beneath if someone passed that way, and then rise up again later.

The water currents also carry with them a large number of fish, large and small, brought from the lakes. They are mostly Catla and Catfish from what the locals have told me (Kendai and Keluthi in Tamil) and also quite a number of the invasive Tilapia fish. The mixing currents at the canal's mouth create little whirlpools in which the fish are caught and tossed into the air by the swirling water. Some are thrown further upstream but others are thrown onto the cement culverts or on the ground above and the fish desperately slap their bodies and tails over the hard surfaces and throw themselves back into the water. Sometime during the day, usually at twilight, the Checkered Keelbacks gather on the cement culverts. They too are familiar of the behavior of the currents and they will lay waiting here with their heads raised, with tense scales, watching eagerly into the stream. As soon as a fish is thrown out of the stream, one of the snakes would instantaneously spring forward, grab the fish between its jaws and fall into the water. Then it would swim to banks, swallow the fish and return to its post again. Hardly a fish went by, which wasn't caught by the snakes, if it was tossed out of the water. Whether they were thrown on the ground behind, on the banks or further into the water the snakes would jump like a recoiling spring, forward, backwards, above or sideways and catch them. There were no petty fights over food between the two snakes and both would leave eachother adequate space. Sometimes it seemed like they even took turns.

More than a dozen Rice-field Crabs (Oziotelphusa species) as well had their abodes by the canal. And they too would come to these culverts to fish. They would stand sideways at the mouth of the culverts all day and dip their pincers into the water, holding them wide open and hoping to catch some little fry which may happen to pass through. They would perpetually be waiting in this fashion and I would often forget that they even existed. Once in a very long while, one of the crabs would have finally managed to catch a small fish. Or it was more likely that it had only managed to nip off the fish's tail or the latter half of its unbleeding translucent body. Immediately a clumsy brawl breaks out and the rest of the crabs scuttle to the lucky one to snatch away its meal. The tiny piece of fish is shred into a further ten pieces and during this game of tug-of war, a few of the crustaceans are pushed into the stream and washed away. The snakes leave space for the quarrelling crabs, slide aside and continue fishing in a corner. In sometime the crabs observe that the serpents are filling their stomachs to a much greater extent than their whole clan put together. Rattling with hunger and jealousy, some of them walk near the snakes and begin nudging them and pinching their flanks with their pincers. Then more join in, in the effort to oust the snakes and to claim the entire canal to themselves. When the crabs turn a real nuisance, the snakes leave the culvert and go into the water or move up onto the land. There is an abundance of fish and frogs during these months and these reptiles can hunt them anywhere. And as long as the water runs with force in these canals, the Checkered Keelbacks and the crabs gather for sometime almost every day on these culverts to catch fish.

Checkered Keelbacks are used to the people of the village and the people here are used to this snake. If the locals crossed paths with one, they would tell each other 'hey it is just a water snake' and will give it its space and will go their way. You will find this snake around any catchment of water and they often will live in a single well or a pond for many years or probably their whole lives. Near paddyfields especially they are fond of waiting inside irrigation channels, swimming against the water's flow, for fish and tadpoles brought with it, straight to their mouths. This snake is not particularly the shy or vigilant type. Ofcourse it will slither away without second thought if it stumbled upon one of us, but it isn't excessively petrified of us either. Especially when it has caught a sizeable frog, which it would like to send down its gullet. Now a frog which has been grabbed by a snake forgets its loud ostentatious croak, which probably gave it up in the first place, and mews and yelps like a kitten, at a high pitch, as if it is pleading for mercy. During the weekend long walks with the children, if we happened to hear this, we would locate the snake and gather around it to watch the scene for a while. The snake would least care about whom or how many were watching it and seldom makes any move to a place with more privacy to consume its meal. It stays put with its sole focus on moving its stretchy mouth over the frog. If the frog is a big one, sometimes the ordeal can take upto an hour so we watch as long as it interests us and then resume our walk. And after a large sized meal the snake is in a dreamy and dazed state and if you don't make way for it once it is done, it will crawl right over your foot and move on, searching for a secluded spot to digest its meal.

But at other times, a cornered or provoked Checkered Keelback can be the most aggressive snake you will come across. It will flatten its throat and strike repeatedly, striking always to bite. And it is a snake which even Irula snake catchers (traditional snake catching tribes from South India) prefer not to pick up, for it never calms down with any amount of proper handling and will repeatedly keep nailing one's hands. One particular Checker, not a very big one, my colleague and I, would see crossing the path leading to our dormitory everyday early in the morning crossing from the southern side of the campus to the northern side. And probably sometime during the evening or the night it came back here. It resided somewhere behind our dorm for we would find it basking on the plinth at dawn break and then moving to where there was more water and better hunting grounds. One morning my colleague suddenly felt like giving the snake a nudge with a cane he happened to be carrying around. It stopped in its tracks, turned to my colleague and lunged at him and actually gave him a chase for a few feet, whilst making successive lunges. Its tongue oscillated with an annoyed rapidity, for having been subjected to such indignation. Then it slid past us again on its routine course.

Sometimes Checkered Keelbacks live long enough to reach an enormous girth. The most massive one I have come across is at the village lake just outside the campus. It lived around one extremity of the lake and would always be sighted there and not anywhere else on the lake's periphery. A large dead palm trunk, hollowed out by ants and termites and smoothened by many years of rain, lay at the lake's edge here and the snake used it to bask in the mornings. It was a real giant for its species. It would have been about a metre and a half in length and had the girth of a modestly sized Rock Python. The chessboard checkered pattern on its back had become hazy with its growth and made it almost unrecognizable. On seeing me it would throw itself off the tree trunk and dig its trails deeply into the soft sand bank as it side-winded towards the water with great effort, making a loud splash as it entered. And then the whole length of the fifteen foot palm trunk it was resting on would be left feebly rotating to and fro on the sand.

Still lake…
ripples from a watersnake
touch the shore

THE ALARMS OF LAPWINGS

SUMMER'S DUSK. I WAS SPRAWLED ACROSS ALL of the three stairs outside my dormitory correcting a mountainous heap of term end test papers. The sun had set and a red full moon was rising gloomily over the Palm trees in the distance. The wind had a whiff of freshly watered and ploughed clay from the fields. It was the most conducive environment for doing work. However I progressed very little with the papers as a Red-Wattled Lapwing was circling in the air above me with half-hearted wing beats, shrieking rudely and eyeing me with a tilted head. I got up and looked around for a possible source for its restlessness; say a dog trotting in the grass where the bird was planning to retire for the night, a Jackal stalking field mice on silent paws or a couple of my students secretly playing cricket on the other side of the dorm, instead of sitting inside and doing homework. On this occasion I couldn't find any source of disturbance and didn't understand why the bird was screaming with such frenzy. It was unreasonable ofcourse for it to protest about my presence; here I was well within my jurisdiction minding my own business. In a fit, I got up, waved my hands at it and gave out a yell, hoping to chase it from right overhead but the creature made louder demonstrations. It continued to shower its abuses for the next half hour till I got up and went for dinner after which it abruptly quietened down and settled somewhere in the darkness of the grass fields. What did the lapwing see in me to yell so vehemently? People say that animals, especially dogs could sense your wicked thoughts and foul intentions when you had them during when they would bark at you very unusually. Did the bird see something dark in me that evening? I couldn't help wondering.

On many other nights I have laid sleepless on my bed, tormented by the distress calls of a Lapwing outside my window, which is demonstrating against some nocturnal perpetrator. It would probably be quarter a mile away but the cold air would carry the sound unattenuated. In Tamil it is aptly named 'Aal-kaati-kuruvi' which loosely translates to 'the bird which gives away the presence of man.' The bird spends its waking hours foraging by cultivations, water bodies and sufficiently green pastures along with other birds. But the Lapwing keeps an alert stance, a watchful eye and never lets down its guard. You will never see it ever lapse into a reposeful mood or its eyelids even briefly shut for rest. Its job all round the clock is to warn the rest of the bird community of any approaching threats, much like the Go-away birds of Africa. The other birds take their cue when it is sounded and flee. But in a few instances I have surely seen the Red-Wattled Lapwing give a false alarm, when there is thick competition for morsels in a feeding ground, and then making the most of its brief deception.

So many too are the times when this bird has turned out to be a nuisance on my birding walks. I would chance upon something rare, something I had been awaiting the whole year to observe or to get a picture for the record, and the Lapwing would screech and send it away before any of it could happen. I vividly recount a walk I had in the Paalar river basin years back. It was late in August that from a tall mound of quarried sand I had spotted a large flock of Garganeys which were vigorously grooming themselves in a reed ridden pool of water some distance away. Now these migrant ducks were an early flock and the first I had seen of the year. In these parts they feel very insecure, for the water bodies are small and the dense marsh reeds may have anything lurking in them, hence they will find the smallest sound or suspicion, reason to fly away and relocate in a far off part of the basin. So I took a circuitous route through the reed beds, losing my way several times, scaring many a Purple heron and Bittern. By then the sun had begun to set and now I had the ducks within my camera's proximity but blocked away by a thick row of reeds. Kneeling down, I could wedge a gap enough through the vegetation for a view of the ducks. A Lapwing standing on a boulder to my far right had been eyeing me all along with a cocked head and found my activities all too suspicious. At the right moment it flew up and blew the whistle. All the ducks took off together, without even bothering to question its discretion, without even knowing why it was shouting or what the threat was. And all I got was a clear shot of dilating ripples for the record.

I don't bear a grudge on the bird however, despite all the fiascos it has caused for me, for many are also the instances when its alarm calls have guided me to spot a snake or a raptor in the close vicinity.

A more quiet and unforthcoming cousin of the Red Wattle is the Yellow-Wattled Lapwing. Their wattles hang on their beaks like the moustache of a Soviet leader. They are also happily social birds and are fond of spending time in little groups. Dry and scrubby habitats are their haven. On the way back from long walks on scorching May afternoons, with a parched mouth, in spite of emptying a two litre bottle, I have come across these Lapwings foraging about in brittle dry grass which are quivering in the heat waves.

Protest is the Yellow Wattle's last resort. It is more likely that it will stand stone still till you pass or covertly tip-toe behind nearby vegetation if you haven't noticed it. In little flocks they are much bolder and will throw taunts at you from a distance, one after another. If you stumble upon a lone Lapwing, don't make eye contact! Look down immediately and pretend you haven't seen it. It will buy the act. Then pace away to a comfortable distance from where you can sit down and observe the bird and it will not mind you at all.

When nesting however, Yellow-wattled Lapwings are quite aggressive birds. A nesting Red Wattle may only circle the air and screech to distract you from the direction of its nest. But the Yellow Wattles will gang up and execute repeated dive-bomb attacks on the hostile. The lakes near Pathashaala would host several families of Yellow Wattles when they go dry. Don, my companion dog, and I would frequently go walking down the dry lake beds, along the bullock cart tracks which traverse through its length. The farmers would take a shortcut through the lake to their village than go by the protracted roadway. Don likes to intermittently wander off into the tall rough grass on either side of the tracks, chase a Hare or two, scratch his back on a termite hill and then rejoin with me further ahead. But during the nesting months of the Lapwings, if he even stepped into the grass, three or four adult Yellow Wattles would swoop down at him and screech sharply in his ears one after another. I think my dog too could discern when these birds nested for during then, he would trot closely by me unexploratively like he was on a leash, for that particular stretch of the lake.

To complete the list of the Lapwing brethren occurring in this part of the country, the Grey-Headed lapwing certainly requires mention. It hails from China and Japan, but takes the long journey to our country during the winters. Here it takes sanctum in open wetlands and rice cultivations. It can be seen in pairs and trios, methodically stalking the slush for its grubs but it roosts in large flocks along with Godwits, Stilts, Ruffs and other fellow migrants. At the Pallikaranai marsh in Chennai, one can see this bird in particularly large numbers. The Grey-Headed Lapwing has a dull grey overcoat which would make it easily be overlooked if not for its corn yellow legs and beak, and deep bloodshot eyes. In character though, the Grey-Head contrasts greatly with any of its native counter parts. It is a silent and timid bird which goes about its errands without seeking any trouble or entering into any quarrels with the residents of the place. As a migrant, the bird has no reason here to assert its dominion. It is just waiting, just keeping up and keeping alive for these few months till winter passes in its homeland. So maybe for now the bird is wearing a polite and reserved demeanor in a foreign land, having left its rougher edges and breeding anxieties back at home.

THE BIG HEADED CATERPILLAR

I WAS IN THE BATHROOM, ON A WEEKEND morning, taking bath, when a student from my dormitory vehemently knocked on the door, insisting that I come out immediately. He had found yet another new caterpillar on some tree outside the dorm and he claimed that it was the strangest one he had ever seen. Now this is the consequence of calling yourself a naturalist and being a teacher at the same time. My workspace in the staffroom was no pleasant sight and was to the dismay of all my colleagues. The children would bring me all odds and ends they would find all around the wilderness of the campus and pile them up on my table. Snake skins atleast four or more, droppings of birds, caterpillars and reptiles carefully collected in bottle caps, egg shells, insect carapaces, butterfly wings, bones and teeth which could have made a whole skeleton, pupae and feathers from every bird in the land, enough of them if I ever wished to be Icarus someday. And every now and then a child would walk in, grab my hand and drag me outside to a plant or a tree to show something he or she has found on it. Now I should confess that some of the most interesting findings and unusual observations have come to me this way, pointed out by children, out of their ceaseless curiosity.

This boy, on weekends, while his comrades played carom in the common room or sat around the music player, he would sit by a tree outside the dorm and look under every single leaf, in search of bugs and caterpillars, with the thrill and sense of adventure of a sailor exploring uncharted seas. On this occasion he clutched my hand, while I clutched onto the towel around my hip, and hauled me to the man sized Jamun tree growing right outside the backdoor of the dormitory. Now this caterpillar, nibbling ardently on the tender most leaf at the very tip of a branch, had a bulbous green head half the volume of its body. No other feature on it mattered. Imagine a caterpillar from the world of aliens in 'War of the Worlds' and you have an idea of its distinctly disproportionate head. Its body ended with a short tail pointed upwards like that of a pet Doberman. Now whether such a head helped it merge with the large infected tubercles on the Jamun leaves or whether it was due to its large brain size and somehow a vastly superior intellect compared to other larvae, like my comrade was suggesting, we wondered. He was quite pleased to know that this creature was new to me and after searching together we found quite a number of them. The larger larvae nibbled entire leaves, moving their mouth parts from edge of the leaf to the other and on reaching the end, flipping their heads back to the other side like starting a new line on a typewriter, to nibble away a fresh segment. But the smaller ones gnawed only the leaf's top most layer and left behind a thin transparent cuticle beneath, like how a squirrel gnaws out only a coconut's white flesh and leaves behind the shell and its teeth marks.

After searching through the annals of Natural history I discovered that this was the caterpillar of the Carea subtilis, a moth who is among the principal pests and defoliators of the Jamun tree (Syzygium cumini), but we called it the Big headed caterpillar. And apparently, gigantic heads were a feature of all larvae from the Nolidae family of moths, to which this one too belonged. I took a cutting of the tree with the caterpillar and planted it in the soil inside a large glass jar and before I could put a cloth on it, the caterpillar absconded and hence I went out and got another cutting. Jamun cuttings survive long enough in well watered soil, just like Drumstick and Hill Neem cuttings, and therefore one doesn't need to bring in the whole plant to rear their caterpillars nor keep replacing them on fresh branches.

The big-head was a very sensitive creature. When a few of us would gather around and peer into its jar to watch what it was doing, it would feel the warmth of our breaths filling the container and would stop eating immediately. It would then walk away from the leaf it was on, climb down the stalk, then to another twig, go beneath the leaf, walk back up again and repeat over and over. Sauntering all over the plant was its response to perceived threats, with wide effusive nostrils. Camouflage wasn't very much one of its strengths for on its leaf one can spot it as easily as a fly in a milk vessel. And it seems to know well that it wouldn't be very wise of it to freeze in its location like most of its other caterpillar brethren, who wear more cryptic coats and have more modestly sized heads. And therefore it wanders within the foliage at a fairly quick pace to make itself a less easy target for a Bulbul or a Warbler probing its beak in between the leaves.

This was September, a month with mild rains, rainbows, dawns with pink skies and days with puffy cotton ball clouds. A Red ant colony had sniffed the arriving monsoons I suppose, or their former nesting place had been ravaged, and the entire lot decided to move into my room's wall. Their soldiers paraded the vertices of my room at all times and my windows too, carrying back chunks of all the dead insects on the sill. I couldn't leave a biscuit or a bitten apple on my table unattended for even a minute, for there would always be scouts everywhere sniffing around for the smallest crumb that I may leave behind. Some days back these ants had gotten into one of my jars and devoured some Sawfly larvae and the survivors had jumped off their leaves and crouched into the soil. Then onwards I started keeping a plate of water under my jars to prevent the ants from killing my caterpillars. But that day I happened to go for lunch, having forgotten to keep water beneath the Big head's jar. When I came back to my room I saw ant files promptly going in and heading out of the jar. It is a painful thing when a life dies in your responsibility. The ants were all over the Jamun cutting inside and also on a leaf I saw the Big head, chomping away, very much alive. Then what were the ants doing in there, if what they were after wasn't the caterpillar? It was almost an hour since I kept the jar in my room. Now a few ants strayed away from the troop, went onto the caterpillar's leaf and gave it a nip on its rear. Instantly the Big head regurgitated a few drops of green liquid on the ants and rushed away to another leaf. Now a whole horde of ants came over to this leaf and attended to the larva's vomit. They relished it like it was honey and to me it smelt like sweet concentrated Jamun sap. And the next time too when the Big head was discovered elsewhere on the plant it spat out some more juice to lure the ants away from it and then fled. Now was the Big head's big head for storing a large volume of Jamun juice and to escape ants? I put the caterpillar in a different jar over a plate of water before it ran out of vomit.

When it can grow no more and eat no more, the Big-head finds itself two closely spaced leaves and stitches itself in between them with silk from its mouth. Then as it goes into repose, its exterior skin turns into white fluff while its inner body hardens into the pupa. Now from then on, in the mornings, at nights, lunch breaks and tea breaks, we come to the glass jar and peer in between the two Jamun leaves to see if the caterpillar has transformed, whether it has emerged, whether it is still there or has already flown away in the form of a moth. Was it still alive? How long would we have to wait? What would the moth of such a strange caterpillar look like? Would it too have an oversized head? On the sixth night when I brought the jar out to the verandah the moth had already crawled out of its cocoon and was sitting upright on a curled leaf, with damp wings. It had a small flat hairy tail, two thin wiry antennae, as thin as hair and two large black eyes. The moth was about the size of my thumb nail and was as non-descript as the caterpillar was strange. A few minutes was all that we saw it, was all the time that it stayed and then the moth zipped into the night.

What stays with me like a rare souvenir, a precious shard of memory, was my young companion's question to me, he who found the creature, after the moth took flight that night. How does a moth know that it can fly when for so long it was a caterpillar? Indeed how does a creature crawling and hiding under leaves all this while, having spent all its life on a single branch on some extremity of a tree, know what its wings can do, what they are meant for when it suddenly acquires them. How does such a total transformation of body and consciousness take place? Not in terms of genes and proteins or any theory or explanation. What does it really mean, what does it imply within one, to undergo a complete transformation, to burn all our old bridges, to shed away all our previous ways of living, to emerge from a cocoon, to be reborn, to see all the world in an entirely new light?

ON A MARSH HARRIER'S PLATTER

DECEMBER MORNING. THAT IS WHAT I HAPPENED to put down in bold writing in my diary. That day I was accompanying a colleague, on a walk all along the campus fence of Pathashaala.

Through the moderate veil of mist one could see the shapes of the Palm trees all along the village lake nearby. The monsoon rains had given us a brief respite and each of our steps went several inches deep into the soggy and clayey soil. At times a Prosopis thorn would be secretly lodged deep under the wet clay and would impale our tender moist unsuspecting feet like pins into a soft board. Crab holes had appeared ubiquitously all of a sudden like proverbial mole hills and each crab busied itself by carrying mud out of its lair even when they were fully inundated. Here and there beside a crab hole, a Snipe sat as still as a stone, waiting to thrust its bill when the owner emerged out. These are wary birds that would only spot you coming from a stone's throw away and cover low in the grass. When you walk too near for its liking, the bird will swerve into flight in the opposite direction, on vocalizing a petrified squawk! Infact I have not heard or known of it utter any other call than this monosyllabic alarm. On our stroll, we happened to scare a few of these anxious creatures, making them fly in the direction of the lake. But in less than a minute they came returning in an even more frightful state and flew towards the other horizon. Some more joined them a few moments later and at the same time a Lapwing started to screech not far away.

On the other side of the fence was a long patch of thick Vettiver grass (Vetiveria zizanioides), waist high or more, continuing along the Northern boundary of the campus. Through the interstices, one could track the motion of a raptor gliding low among the grass tops. This was a Marsh harrier's beat of course and apparently this bird wakes earlier than most of its kind. This was a female which I had started seeing from around early September over these grounds. We stood still and watched it going by.

It rose up a few feet and glided along at a slow pace between leisurely wing strokes. Quite often with a tilted head, it surveyed the earth below. At times it would match the wind's force and hang stationary for a while. More snipes flew and also a sandpiper or two, but the raptor didn't seem interested in them in the least. Witnessing another Lapwing's protest ahead, the Harrier moved on to the adjacent paddyfields. And there too it continued to ceaselessly fly, and flushing more birds; Egrets, Sandpipers and other waders, but it didn't hone in on any of them. Some of the birds which were foraging in the paddyfields seemed to sense the passive intentions of the Harrier and stayed put even when the predator flew closely above. Birds do very often exhibit this innate understanding of a predator's current intentions. Elsewhere, in large marshlands, I have seen Harriers on their hunting sorties rally hundreds of frightened water birds from one end of the water body to another. While at a different point of time one may see a completely placid individual sitting closely alongside a flock of ducks, which would be perfectly at ease, as if it was one of their own kin.

This particular bird we were watching clearly wasn't going to kill. Its relaxed and serene temperament was evident in the way it buoyantly ambled over the fields. This was very difficult to explain though, from the textbook perspectives used to usually make sense of animal behavior. Probably this bird too was simply taking a morning walk just like us, witnessing the sunrise, feeling the cold wind, breathing the air and just being. There are few things more meditative than a morning walk. As Muir stated "I only went out for a walk and finally concluded to stay out till sundown, for going out, I found, was really going in." We watched the harrier's flight till it got completely enshrouded in the mist beyond.

Some days back I had seen this bird in the lake bed, floating over the grasses in the evening. This was its kingdom till the end of winter and during twilight if one walked along the periphery of the lake, one would definitely chance upon it. That day it seemed to specifically fancy the large green grasshoppers there for I had seen it grasp an airborne one in its talons and then twist and tumble down to have it on the ground. Later on it did the same antics and fell into the grass again. On other occasions it would land directly over some quarry on the ground, with its talons stretched and tail fanned out and I assume it must be some ground borne creature say a mouse, a skink or a loud bull frog, which itself gave away its location. And at other times it hunts ducks and other water birds.

At the Perumbakkam marsh at Chennai, I once chanced upon two Marsh harriers which were team hunting. They rallied hundreds of Shovellers, Garganeys, Teals and other ducks around the marsh, trying to single out one for a kill. Some little flocks flew out of the premises over the side walk and into the city, considering it wise to find another water body to settle in. But most of the ducks flew from one part of the marsh to the other, settling on the waters briefly till the raptors came close and then taking off again and swerving in a different direction, hoping that the predators would soon get exhausted. But one Garganey began falling off from its flock and one of the harriers grabbed it in the air and slammed it on a tiny islet in the middle of the wetland. The other gave up its chase and flew back to its companion to claim its share of the quarry. However, this one which now was busy feathering the duck, had a change of mind and when its partner arrived, it flew to it, clawed and squealed at it, till it was forced to a retreat without a scrap to eat. Now with a full duck to itself, it sat in the grass and began pulling out and swallowing what looked like the intestines from afar, now and then coughing up and spitting out down-feathers. And after having its fill, it sat by what was left of the carcass with a noticeable bigger belly, for the next whole hour digesting its meal.

The Marsh harrier's vast diet fascinated my colleague the most, from all that I had narrated. He saw the bird as a symbol of acceptance, and of contentment. He shared with a tone of wonder that our days too would be so much more leisurely if we accepted and were thankful for whatever life had to offer us for that day, that moment.

The Marsh harrier is also a great opportunist and never misses a chance for freebooting and piracy. When the plough tractor is done with churning over the fields, usually it is the Terns, the Drongos and Bee-Eaters which attend to the uncovered grubs. On occasion I have seen the Harrier arrive late in the scene and join the feast, not so much picking morsels by itself than scaring the Terns and snatching away their catch. But how much ever it wants to stay in the scene, it makes an early departure as the drongos assert their dominion and mob it away.

There are other occasions when the raptor exploits the situation with its opportunism. Later that March, the village lake went dry and one afternoon a huge fire raged in it, consuming the dry grass and all the vegetation. By the evening, the winds were carrying with them constant draughts of burnt flakes and soot from the lake into villages nearby. I had gone to the site just to see the magnitude of the calamity. The dry bed had hosted a large herd of Blackbuck and a numerous scrubland birds. The story which circulated was that some ignorant villager had dropped his beedi (the local cigarette) and walked away and this had sparked the fire. A more sinister tale was that the local sand mafia had deliberately set fire to the lakebed to make a path for their bullock carts to carry their loads through the village. The fire spanned several acres and the daily evening chorus of Jackals howling, Thick knees hooting and Francolins calling were replaced by the thunderous crackling of giant flames. The only organism to be seen however was the Marsh harrier, flying alone along the fire's periphery and at times swooping in right above the flames in pursuit of something. Now and then it executed a short dive or a twist, catching a grasshopper or a beetle or whatever it was which was attempting to escape the blazes. And then it quartered about patiently till the next insect flew out. Even as twilight faded into darkness, the bird continued to hawk the insects and saunter over the scorching air, in the glow of the dying flames.

EYES ON THE OLEANDER

THE ACADEMIC TERM WAS NEARLY COMING TO an end and all of us teachers had our noses buried in writing student reports, correcting checkpoint papers, managing classes and preparing students for the term end programme. We ate, breathed and slept during the narrow interstices of time in between. As with the student reports, some were still struggling against the resistance to put pen to paper or finger to keyboard while others slogged day and night to be quickly done with the considerable workload. An interruption to my report writing came as a boy who banged on the staffroom window and asked me whether I had seen the huge caterpillars on the Oleander plants. Two Oleander saplings which were planted at either side of the entrance to the classroom block about four years back were now shoulder high plants. And this time of the year, every year, there would be a profuse number of caterpillars of the Common Crow butterflies on these plants. So I asked the boy not to linger around and return to his class soon. But the word 'huge' kept hanging on my mind for a while and I got up for a small stroll around the Oleanders. A necessary break!

Many girls and boys had also gathered around the two plants. Chomping away at the apical red flower clusters were large parrot green caterpillars, longer than the length of my fingers. This was the first year we saw the Oleander Hawk moth's (Daphnis nerii) caterpillars inside the campus and I knew this for sure as these saplings have been under gaze everyday from the day they were brought in black plastic packs from a nursery. Elsewhere in the villages outside, I would come across them often and have even considered introducing a few on the plants in school. I haven't however. This year the Hawk moths by themselves had deemed these plants worthy enough to lay their eggs. There were also a dozen or more Crow larvae too on each of the plants and their bright golden pupae hung under several of the leaves, like shiny Christmas Eve decorations. Along the sides of the Hawk moth larvae ran two thick bluish-white lines, making their large bodies surprisingly merge with the crowd of thick midribs of the Oleander leaves. The little black specks on each of their body's segments, over every spiracle, reminded me of windows on a train carriage. They raptly nibbled away on the petals completely oblivious to the hubbub the children were making around them, until a girl accidently poked one with her finger while pointing at it.

As the caterpillar tucked in its head deep into its neck flesh, as it curled its fore body forward into a question mark, folds of skin on its upper back straightened out and revealed two large ghoulish eyes. There were gasps of excitement. These were no real eyes ofcourse; its actual ones are only rudimentary light sensitive ovals right at the tip of its head. But these were phony ones which it used in defense to scare away anything which poked or prodded it, with whatever intention in mind. The eyes had a black outline, as if sketched with an artist's pen, melding inwards into deep glowing blue and then ending with pale white centres. Seen in the moonlight, they could have been the cold lifeless eyes of the walking dead or the sinister eyes of a small apparition.

On a grimmer note, the most common devices of suicide among depressed youths in the village are the seeds of the Oleander plant. I myself have seen a couple of victims during my trips to the nearby government hospital, frothing copiously at the mouth as a result of the poisoning. And all the larvae which have evolved to eat the Oleander's leaves, store this poison in them, making themselves lethal as well. They may too be fatal for all those which may consider a caterpillar for a quick snack. And to prevent all this mutual damage these Hawk moth caterpillars warn their attackers by uncovering their eerie eye spots.

The children would wait till the caterpillar felt that the disturbance had passed, folded its back flaps, pulled out its head and resumed nibbling on the plant. Then they would prod its face again and it would curl up and repeat its antics. After a few times of showing off its aposematic displays, the caterpillar would get fed up and would either reverse itself and walk to a different leaf, or would ignore any subsequent pokes. Some children made it a point to poke a caterpillar each time they went in or out of the classroom block.

As October went by, the monsoon holidays commenced. More rains came and many more caterpillars appeared on the Oleanders. On some days, during the dim twilight hours I have seen the blur of a Hawk moth whiz away after depositing its eggs on the plant. I found their caterpillars later on the Gardenia plants near the administration office too. Something was different about this year. There were a few more caterpillar species which I found had immigrated into the campus this season, which were never spotted before. The horned and grainy skinned Black Rajah caterpillars on the Madras Thorn Trees for instance. When the floods of December 2015 hit us a month later I couldn't help wondering whether the profusion of larvae earlier was in anyway correlated with the disaster. Hindsight often proves misleading, but was it possible that the insects sensed the calamitous rains months back and hence expanded their territories to drier regions in the neighborhood, knowing that the coming year would be much greener?

I took some cuttings to my room to rear these creatures and watch them closely. While they were there, I delegated the work of bringing fodder for the larvae to the students of my dorm. But during the holidays the walk from the dorm to the Oleander plants would be nearly a kilometer in the hundred acre campus.

On reaching its full size, the green skin of the caterpillar starts turning wrinkly and creased, like old black date prunes. Then it starts turning brown and orange, and it begins moving groggily down the plant and partially buries itself under the soil in the jar. Now this is something to remember in your garden when you are treading around the host plants of Hawk moths that many may be pupating just beneath the mud. Within hours the old skin is shed away to one end and the organism is now cased by a hard pupal shell with a sticky surface which makes mud adhere to it. Now during my first rearing I was an eager student and every morning and night I would shove aside some earth and see if the moth has emerged. The annoyed mass of life would wriggle its abdomen back and forth and dig deeper into the soil. It is interesting how completely defenseless pupae too employ some methods to protect themselves. Many squirm and wriggle so much that it is impossible to get a grip on them. Crow pupae can rattle themselves if touched. And once the caterpillar of a Moth from the Hulodes genus got into my spare bed sheet and began pupating. It was like the creature's posterior end was stitched into the cloth, for it was an extremely hard task to remove it. And when I did manage to, strands of thread were pulled away along with the pupa. I kept it over a handkerchief on my table and in the next few hours the tip of the pupa were grabbing the strands of the kerchief as well. A closer look disclosed that this pupa kept growing a long network of minuscule hooks at the very tip of its abdomen which grew around and grappled onto the threads of the fabric. I also found these creatures pupating in folded Shamianas and curtains used once in several months. Was this a moth which had evolved to pupate in pieces of cloth we periodically forget about?

On the eleventh or the twelfth night, you can remain awake near your jar in which the Oleander Hawk moth is metamorphosing, for almost surely by this time you can see the wings, eyes and body of the moth having fully formed within the cocoon and the moth is very likely to emerge by now. It too is Green but the green of an army uniform. Its wings extending from its torso look like those of a fighter jet. Now take another good look at it and it may seem like an entirely different thing. The two black spots under its head look like eyes, its wide flat wings seem like ears and its thick segmented body resembles a trunk and the whole upper side of the moth looks remarkably like the face of an elephant or more closely, how the Hindu elephant God, Vinayagar, is sometimes depicted. The moth walks around like a toddler for a while, on its new found legs. I then carry it out to my verandah and give it something to perch on and dry its wings under the solar lamp. When it decides to fly, in a bat of an eye it is gone.

During my walks in the late evenings, I often stop by and smell the white blossoms of a Jasmine plant or a Nona plant by the side of the road, the scents of which are much stronger as the night begins to settle. Sometimes I am accompanied by the soft buzz of an Oleander Hawk moth hovering above me as it attends to the flowers, which too has been invited by the same aroma.

Bully Ants and Gram Blues – Devout companions, the Ant and the Caterpillar

The Wolves among Snakes – The Wolf snake on the loft

The Wolves among Snakes – A Barred Wolf snake coiling up on being spotted

Gulls and Terns – A Gulls chases a Tern, intent on snatching its catch

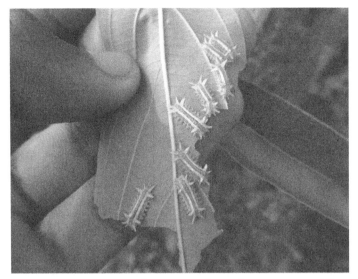

Itches, Inflammations and other Caterpillar defenses – The infamous Nettle Moth Caterpillars

Itches, Inflammations and other Caterpillar defenses – The aggressive Semi-Looper larvae, large and small

Hopes for a Vanishing Marshland – A Pheasant Tailed Jacana in its breeding plumes

Of Blackbuck Herds – A family herd through the morning mist

Of Blackbuck Herds – A bachelor duo, a senior and a youngster

Wings in the Skies – A Black Rajah mud puddles in wet gravel, cement and clay

Wings in the Skies – Common Line Blues attending fresh cow pat

The Drama of Kukris – A Banded Kukri pretending to be a Viper

The Drama of Kukris – A Russell's Kukri having just jumped from a crevice in the brickwork

Of the Milkweed Community – A mating pair of adult Painted Grasshoppers

Francolin Calls – A Francolin pair enjoying a gravel bath

Residing with Signature Spiders – A Signature Spider in a Science Park

Fisherfolk of the Culverts – A Bullfrog for breakfast

The Alarms of Lapwings – A Red Wattle eyeing with suspicion

The Alarms of Lapwings – A gang on Yellow Wattles

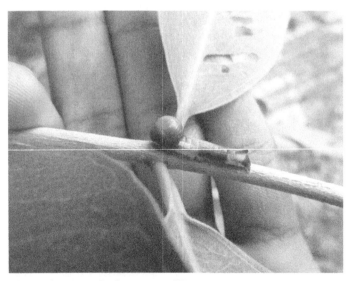

The Big Headed Caterpillar – The Big head (Carea subtilis) on a Jamun branch

On a Marsh Harrier's platter – A sauntering Harrier

Eyes on the Oleander – Its phony eyes

Eyes on the Oleander – The little hooks on the tip of a pupa from the Hulodes genus

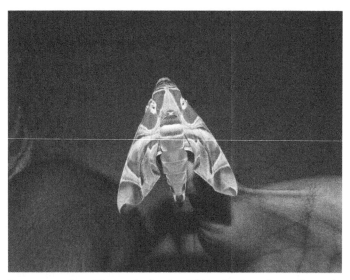

Eyes on the Oleander – An Oleander Hawk Moth ready to fly

Made in United States
Orlando, FL
12 January 2024

42404019R00146